Protocols for Paleontological Resource Site Monitoring at Zion National Park

Natural Resource Report NPS/ZION/NRR—2012/595

Erica C. Clites

Glen Canyon National Recreation Area
P O Box 1507
Page, AZ 86040

Vincent L. Santucci

National Park Service
Geologic Resources Division
1201 Eye Street NM
Washington DC 20005

November 2012

U.S. Department of the Interior
National Park Service
Natural Resource Stewardship and Science
Fort Collins, Colorado

The National Park Service, Natural Resource Stewardship and Science office in Fort Collins, Colorado publishes a range of reports that address natural resource topics of interest and applicability to a broad audience in the National Park Service and others in natural resource management, including scientists, conservation and environmental constituencies, and the public.

The Natural Resource Report Series is used to disseminate high-priority, current natural resource management information with managerial application. The series targets a general, diverse audience, and may contain NPS policy considerations or address sensitive issues of management applicability.

All manuscripts in the series receive the appropriate level of peer review to ensure that the information is scientifically credible, technically accurate, appropriately written for the intended audience, and designed and published in a professional manner.

This report received formal peer review by subject-matter experts who were not directly involved in the collection, analysis, or reporting of the data, and whose background and expertise put them on par technically and scientifically with the authors of the information.

Views, statements, findings, conclusions, recommendations, and data in this report do not necessarily reflect views and policies of the National Park Service, U.S. Department of the Interior. Mention of trade names or commercial products does not constitute endorsement or recommendation for use by the U.S. Government.

This report is available from the Natural Resource Publications Management website (http://www.nature.nps.gov/publications/nrpm/).

Please cite this publication as:

Clites, E. C. and V. L. Santucci. 2012. Protocols for paleontological resource site monitoring at Zion National Park. Natural Resource Report NPS/ZION/NRR—2012/595. National Park Service, Fort Collins, Colorado.

NPS 116/117670, November 2012

Contents

Contents (continued)

Figures

Appendices

Executive Summary

The rock exposures in Zion National Park (Zion NP) record 300 million years of Earth's history, and most of the sedimentary rock units contain fossils. Zion NP has over 160 documented paleontological localities comprising vertebrate (bone and teeth), invertebrate (marine and freshwater molluscs), plant (permineralized wood) and trace fossils (dinosaur trackways, invertebrate burrows). These 21 sites were selected based on the availability of locality data, presence inside the park boundary, mitigation ranking from DeBlieux (2005), susceptibility to natural and human-caused erosion, fossil significance, accessibility, and proximity to other sites. Representative sites from diverse formations and geographic locations are included. This report outlines monitoring protocols for those recommended sites, recommended techniques such as repeat photography and crack monitors, as well as procedures for documenting new sites.

Paleontological resources are non-renewable, and can be very susceptible to impacts from natural erosion and human influences. Once fossil resources are damaged, destroyed, or removed from their original context without proper documentation, their scientific and educational values can never be replaced. Documenting long-term changes in the condition and stability of paleontological resources will provide managers with a warning of the rate and degree of impacts on resources and may provide the scientific basis for future administrative actions for their management.

Santucci et al. (2009) outlines five vital signs for the monitoring of *in situ* paleontological resources. These include: erosion (geologic factors), erosion (climatic factors), catastrophic geohazards, hydrology/bathymetry and human access/public use. The measureable objectives of monitoring include: determining whether the quality of the site's condition (based on the monitoring score) is improving or declining , allowing a resource manager to determine whether the changes are primarily due to natural processes such as erosion or human influence and documenting whether fossils are being exposed and at what rate.

A number of park-specific forms are provided including:

- Paleontological Locality Database Form,

- Paleontological Locality Condition Evaluation Form,

- Paleontological Isolated Find Data Form,

- Trackway Worksheet and

- Paleontological Site Report.

Fieldwork and office procedures are outlined in a series of eight standard operating procedures. These include:

- a job hazard analysis for paleontological fieldwork,

- documenting a new paleontological locality,

- monitoring documented paleontological localities,

- prioritizing paleontological sites for monitoring,

- using a field notebook,

- photographing fossils in the field,

- recording GPS locations in the field and

- data management for paleontological site files.

The materials provided constitute a tool kit that can be adapted for use by any park service area. It should provide a solid starting point for managing fossil resources subject to the "no impairment" standard set forth in the National Park Service Organic Act (1916). The Paleontological Resources Preservation Act (2009) also mandates that paleontological resources on Federal land are managed and protected using scientific principles and expertise.

Acknowledgments

National Park Service staff with paleontological expertise generously responded to a request for site documentation and monitoring guidelines in May 2011. Documents were received from A. Aase (Museum Specialist, Fossil Butte National Monument), G. Bell (Environmental Protection Specialist, Great Basin National Park), R. Benton (Paleontologist, Badlands National Park), P. Gensler (Curator/Paleontologist, Hagerman Fossil Beds National Monument), J. Hearst (Geologist, Guadalupe Mountains National Park), H. Meyer (Paleontologist, Florissant Fossil Beds National Monument), W. Parker (Vertebrate Paleontologist, Petrified Forest National Park), J. Samuels (Curator/Chief of Paleontology, John Day Fossil Beds National Monument) and C. Schierup (Collections Manager, John Day Fossil Beds National Monument). Additional brainstorming discussions took place with G. Bell, D. Greco (Physical Science Program Manager, Grand Canyon National Park) and J. Kenworthy (NPS Geologic Resources Division). Forms included in this report (Appendix B, C, D) were originally designed by M. Miller (GeoCorps of America). The Trackway Worksheet is based on forms provided by A. Milner (Paleontologist/Curator, St. George Dinosaur Discovery Site at Johnson Farm). The Visitor Report Form (Appendix F) is based on a template from Badlands National Park.

Dave Sharrow (Hydrologist, Zion National Park) and Fred Armstrong (Chief of Resource Management and Research, Zion National Park) participated in project discussions and provided helpful feedback. Tim Connors (Geologist, Geologic Resources Division) and Greg McDonald (NPS Senior Curator for Natural History) provided substantive review comments that greatly improved this manuscript. John Spence (Glen Canyon National Recreation Area) allowed the first author to complete the project from her duty station in Page, AZ.

Background and Objectives

Purpose and Organization of the Protocol

This document describes the rationale and methods used by the National Park Service (NPS) for long-term monitoring of paleontological sites and resources at Zion National Park. The monitoring effort will collect data for key metrics representing the health of paleontological resources in Zion NP. Over time, monitoring data will provide an indication of the trend of those metrics and whether park action is required to rectify those situations in which the fossil resources are being degraded. The monitoring then provides park managers with a warning of changes that are occurring, and justifies further administrative action. This narrative portion of the protocol provides background and justification for the monitoring of paleontological resources, as well as brief descriptions of data collection methods and operational procedures (Long and Mitchell 2012). The Standard Operating Procedures (SOPs) that follow the narrative contain the detailed instructions for implementing the protocol. The SOPs begin with a Job Hazard Analysis for paleontological fieldwork; then proceed to specific guidelines for documenting new sites, monitoring natural and human-caused erosion at known sites, field notebook use, photography, GPS and overall data management techniques. The narrative and SOPs are organized and written according to the NPS protocol guidelines (Oakley et al. 2003).

Paleontological Resource Law and Policy

In March 2009, the Paleontological Resource Preservation Act (PRPA) was signed into law (Public Law 111–11). This act defines paleontological resources as "any fossilized remains, traces, or imprints of organisms, preserved in or on the earth's crust, that are of paleontological interest and that provide information about the history of life on earth." The law stipulates that the Secretary of the Interior should manage and protect paleontological resources using scientific principles. The Secretary should also develop plans for "inventory, monitoring, and the scientific and educational use of paleontological resources."

Paleontological resources are considered park resources and values that are subject to the "no impairment" standard in the National Park Service Organic Act (1916). In addition to the Organic Act, PRPA will serve as a primary authority for the management, protection and interpretation of paleontological resources (see Appendix A). Their proper management and preservation should be considered by park resource managers whether or not fossil resources are specifically identified in the park's enabling legislation.

The Paleontological Resources Management section of NPS Reference Manual 77 provides guidance on the implementation and continuation of paleontological resource management programs. Administrative options include those listed below:

No Action - would mean that no action would be taken to collect the fossils as they erode from the strata. The fossils would be left to erode naturally and over time crumble away naturally or possibly be vandalized, either intentionally or unintentionally by visitors.

Surveys - will be set up to document potential fossil localities. All sites will be documented with the use of GPS and will be entered into the park GIS database. Associated stratigraphic and depositional environment information will be collected for each locality. A preliminary faunal list will be developed. Any evidence of poaching activity will be recorded. Rates of erosion will be estimated for the site and a monitoring schedule will be developed based upon this information. A NPS Paleontological Locality Database Form will also be completed for each locality.

Monitoring - would mean that periodically fossil rich areas of Zion NP would be examined to determine if conditions have changed to such an extent that additional management actions are warranted. Photographic records should be kept so that changes can be more easily ascertained.

Cyclic Prospecting- would mean that areas of high erosion which also have a high potential for producing significant specimens should be periodically examined for new sites. The periodicity of such cyclic prospecting will depend on the abundance of fossils and the rate of sediment erosion.

Stabilization and reburial - would mean that significant specimens which cannot be immediately collected may be stabilized using appropriate consolidants and reburied. Reburial slows down, but does not stop the destruction of a fossil by erosion. Therefore, this method would be used only as an interim and temporary stop-gap measure.

Shelter construction - means that fossil sites or specimens which could be exhibited *in situ* will require protective shelters to protect them from the natural forces of erosion. The use of shelters will likely draw attention to the fossils and increase the risk of vandalism or theft. They also provide an opportunity for interpretation and education.

Excavation - means the partial or complete removal of any or all fossils present on the surface and potentially the removal of specimens still beneath the surface which have not been exposed by erosion.

Closure - means that the area containing fossils may be temporarily or permanently closed to the public to protect the fossil resources. Fossil rich areas may be closed to the public unless accompanied by an interpretive ranger on a guided hike.

Patrols - may be increased into areas of known fossil resources. Patrols can prevent and/or reduce theft and vandalism. The scientific community and the public expect the NPS to protect its paleontological resources from vandalism and theft.

National Park Service Management Policies (2006; Section 4.8.2.1) also require that paleontological resources, including both organic and mineralized remains in body or trace form, will be protected, preserved, and managed for public education, interpretation, and scientific research. In 2010, in cooperation with many partners, the National Park Service founded National Fossil Day, a celebration organized to promote public awareness and stewardship of fossils, as well as to foster a greater appreciation of their scientific and educational value (http://nature.nps.gov/geology/nationalfossilday/). At Zion NP, awareness can be raised about fossils by directing visitors to the St. George Dinosaur Discovery Site at Johnson Farm (St. George, UT) and the Grand Staircase-Escalante National Monument.

Rationale for Paleontological Site Monitoring at Zion NP
Zion NP is renowned for its scenic geology of towering sandstone buttes and canyons. The rock exposures of Zion NP record 300 million years of Earth's history, and most of these rock units

are sedimentary units that contain fossils. Fossils contribute to our understanding of the history of life, past ecosystems and evolutionary and climate change over time. Zion NP fossils provide great opportunities for scientific research and for public education of these processes.

In Zion NP, fossils are known from *in situ* occurrences within geologic formations, surficial deposits, in which they may have been transported from their original context, and within a cultural resource context. Paleontological resources are known from the Kaibab, Moenkopi, Chinle, Moenave, Kayenta, Navajo, Carmel, Cedar Mountain and Dakota formations, as well as from Quaternary deposits (Figure 1). Triassic Moenkopi Formation tetrapod tracks in the park represent the second oldest Mesozoic vertebrate tracks in North America (Mickelson et al. 2006). Historically, the Zion NP area has been important for the study of the Triassic Chinle Formation (Stewart et al. 1972), including collections made by E. H. Colbert of the American Museum of Natural History. Consequently the documentation of the park's fossil resources also depends on their long term care in museum collections whether in the park or with non-federal repositories.

At the contact between the Shinarump Conglomerate and the Petrified Forest Member of the Chinle Formation, *Araucarioxylon* and *Woodworthia* petrified logs are sufficiently concentrated to be considered a petrified forest (DeBlieux et al. 2005, 2006). Vertebrate remains known from the Chinle Formation in Zion NP include fish, metoposaurs, aetosaurs, phytosaurs and others (DeBlieux et al. 2005, 2006; Santucci and Kirkland 2010). The Kayenta Formation has the highest concentration of fossils of any of the park's formations (DeBlieux et al. 2006), with dozens of tracksites discovered during field surveys. The top of the Springdale Sandstone Member of the Kayenta is considered a megatracksite that extends throughout southern Utah and northern Arizona (Lucas et al. 2005; Hamblin et al. 2006; Lucas and Tanner 2006; Milner and Spears 2007). Zion NP also contains significant Quaternary lake deposits containing microfossils, plants and mollusks, as well as vertebrate bones and tracks (Tweet et al. 2012).

Fossils are non-renewable resources that are susceptible to a wide range of threats, both natural and human-caused. An ever increasing commercial market for fossils presents challenges to all land managers charged with protecting fossils on public lands. Once fossil resources are damaged, destroyed, or removed from their original context without proper documentation, their scientific and educational values can never be replaced. At Zion NP, the spectacular rate of erosion that exposes rock outcrops and fossils is also a threat to the preservation of those fossils (Tweet et al. 2012). Based on the extent of exposure of an inverted valley with a dated basalt cap, the regional rate of erosion has been estimated at 400 m (1,300 ft.) per million years (Willis and Biek 2001; Biek et al. 2010). In two cases at Zion NP, fossil trackways located on the undersides of hanging ledges have collapsed within two years of their discovery (DeBlieux et al. 2006; Markle 2008; D. Sharrow pers. comm. May 2011).

Long-term monitoring programs represent an important step towards managing these resources. The protocol developed by these programs are intended to ensure that changes detected by monitoring are occurring in nature and not simply a result of measurements taken by different observers or in slightly different ways (Oakley et al. 2003).

SYSTEM	SERIES	FORMATION	MEMBER	SYMBOL	THICKNESS feet (meters)	LITHOLOGY
QUATERNARY	HOLO. and PLEIST.		Surficial Deposits	Qa, QTao, Qms, Taf	0-100 (0-30)	
			Basalt Flows and Cinder Cones	Qbc, Qbg, Qbv, Qbp, Qbl, Qbkp, Qbhr, Qblc	0-500 (0-150)	
CRET.	L. and U.		Cedar Mountain and Dakota Fms. undivided	Kdc	100 (30)	K unconformity
JURASSIC	MIDDLE	CARMEL FM.	Winsor Member	Jcw	180-280 (55-85)	Pale-yellow sandstone
			Paria River Member	Jcp	50-80 (15-24)	"Chippy" limestone / Alabaster
			Crystal Creek Member	Jc Jcx	150-185 (45-55)	"Banded" sandstone
			Co-op Creek Limestone Member — Upper unit	Jccu	100-110 (30-33)	
			Co-op Creek Limestone Member — Lower unit	Jccl	150-170 (45-53)	Isocrinus
		TEMPLE CAP FM.	White Throne Member	Jt Jtw	0-190 (0-58)	J-2 unconformity
			Sinawava Member	Jts	40-60 (12-18)	Red marker / J-1 unconformity / Jointed massive vertical cliffs
	LOWER	NAVAJO SANDSTONE	white subunit	Jnw	0-800 (0-245)	
			pink subunit	Jn Jnp	600-1,000 (180-300)	Local ironstone / High-angle eolian cross-beds
			brown subunit	Jnb	400-600 (120-180)	Vertical cliffs
		KAYENTA FM.	Tenney Canyon Tongue	Jkt	140-315 (43-96)	
			Lamb Point Tongue of Navajo Ss	Jnl	0-120 (0-37)	Sandstone ledge
			Main body	Jk	290-360 (88-110) 550-700 (168-213)	
		MOENAVE FM.	Springdale Sandstone Member	Jks	90-150 (27-46)	Vertical cliff
			Whitmore Point Member	Jm Jmw	60-80 (18-24)	Fish fossils (Semionotus kanabensis)
			Dinosaur Canyon Member	Jmd	175-210 (53-64)	J-0 unconformity
TRIASSIC	UPPER	CHINLE FM.	Petrified Forest Member	Ɍcp	450-500 (135-150)	Variegated or banded slope / "Popcorn" weathering / Covered by landslides
			Shinarump Conglomerate Member	Ɍcs	60-135 (18-41)	Fossil wood / Ɍ-3 unconformity
	LOWER	MOENKOPI FORMATION	upper red member	Ɍmu	275 (85)	"Purgatory Sandstone"
			Shnabkaib Member	Ɍms	300 (90)	Gypsum
			middle red member	Ɍm Ɍmm	200 (60)	
			Virgin Limestone Member	Ɍmv	100 (30)	
			lower red member	Ɍml	160 (50)	
			Timpoweap Member	Ɍmt	30-80 (9-24)	Oil seeps
			Rock Canyon Conglomerate Member	Ɍmr	0-50 (0-15)	Cherty conglomerate / Ɍ-1 unconformity
PERMIAN	LOWER	KAIBAB FM.	Harrisburg Member	Pu Pkh	150-200 (46-60)	Brachiopods / "Black-banded"
			Fossil Mountain Member	Pkf	240 (73)	

Figure 1. Stratigraphic section of Zion National Park, showing geologic units that outcrop in the park and are described in this report (modified from Biek et al. 2003 and presented in Lund et al. 2010).

Protocol Development

Santucci et al. (2009) outlined monitoring methods for *in situ* paleontological resources. Baseline locality information and stressors are used to design a paleontological resource monitoring plan. Weathering and erosion are the primary natural processes that affect *in situ* fossil sites. Fossils may also be disturbed by direct human interference.

In cooperation with the Utah Geological Survey, a National Park Service prototype paleontological monitoring site was set up in Glen Canyon National Recreation Area (GLCA) in 2009-2010. Abundant dinosaur tracks are present at the site, which is affected by natural and human-caused erosion and damage. Many of the techniques outlined in Santucci et al. (2009) were employed at the site, including rebar stakes to mark a photo point and crack monitors. This protocol document is based on two years of site monitoring conducted at GLCA beginning in May 2010.

Measureable Objectives

Santucci et al. (2009) outline five vital signs for the monitoring of *in situ* paleontological resources. These include: erosion (geologic factors), erosion (climatic factors), catastrophic geohazards, hydrology/bathymetry and human access/public use. For each of these vital signs, methods requiring varying expertise from volunteers to scientists are needed to monitor changes.

A fossil site in good condition is one where paleontological resources and their associated geologic context are maintained *in situ* in a stable environment on a human time scale. The fossils are in good condition with little or no potential for degradation or impairment by artificially accelerated natural processes or direct human impacts. Similarly, the scientific and educational values are unimpaired and are also preserved in good condition (Santucci et al. 2009, p. 188).

Monitoring Objectives
- Determine whether site condition (based on total score from Paleontological Locality Condition Evaluation Form) is stable (no observable change) or declining over time scales of five – ten years.

- Determine whether changes taking place are primarily due to natural erosion or human influences.

- Document additional fossils as they are exposed. As appropriate, fossils may be documented through photographs, sketches, site mapping, casting or collection. Contact interested scientists to conduct further research if desired.

- Determine if fossil being exposed are of scientific interest and should be collected as part of park's museum collection.

Programmatic Objectives
- Work with the NPS Division of Interpretation and Education to increase visitor's knowledge of paleontological resources and their protection.

- Work with park museum program on the inclusion of any collected fossils in the park museum collection.

Management Objectives

- Provide baseline data that can be integrated with law and policy in planning and decision-making related to paleontological resources.

- Provide justification for additional administrative actions to preserve paleontological resources unimpaired.

Sampling Design

Site Selection

A documented paleontological locality is a spatially defined area where fossils have been collected in the past or where *in situ* fossils are present (Santucci et al. 2009). The documentation of a fossil site begins with baseline paleontological resource data. Those data include a site description, photographs, and some level of mapping (Fremd 1992). Specific measureable information includes (Santucci et al. 2009):

1) lithology of fossiliferous (fossil-bearing) strata,

2) relationship of overlying and underlying strata,

3) degree of slope of fossiliferous strata,

4) type and percentage of vegetation cover, as well as

5) type, diversity and concentration of fossils within the site.

Sampling Frequency

Important fossil sites should be documented using the NPS Paleontological Locality Database Form, the NPS Paleontological Locality Condition Evaluation Form and the establishment of a photo point. In addition to documenting the site through photographs, mapping and descriptions, the site condition should be monitored every one- to five years to ensure site preservation.

Sites to be Monitored in Zion National Park

Twenty-one sites that have been identified as candidates for monitoring in Zion NP (Markle, 2008) are listed in the following Table. These 21 sites were selected based on the availability of locality data, presence inside the park boundary, mitigation ranking from DeBlieux (2005), susceptibility to natural and human-caused erosion, fossil significance, accessibility, and proximity to other sites. An initial round of monitoring is planned for fall of 2012, after which the list will be revisited and revised as needed.

Site Number	Condition Score	Significance*	Type	Notes
42Ws002t	40	Significant	Trace	This is the "Subway" track site. Along heavily-used trail, Kayenta Formation.
42Ws183t	45	Critical	Trace	Tracks on a loose block which is very susceptible to slides, Kayenta Formation.
42Ws184t	55	Significant	Trace	Tracks on a loose block which is very susceptible to slides, Kayenta Formation.
42Ws188t	65	Significant	Trace	The site is very susceptible to erosion, Moenave Formation, Springdale Member.
42Ws210t	80	Important	Trace	Another trackway site that is susceptible to erosion. It is close to site 42Ws188 and could easily be monitored in conjunction with that site, Kayenta Formation.
42Ws214p	45	Important	Veg	A good representative to monitor natural changes to large well-preserved petrified wood sites in the park, Chinle Formation, Petrified Forest Member.
42Ws222v	15	Significant	Vert	This is one of the best bone and teeth sites in the park. The outcrop is quite susceptible to erosion

Site Number	Condition Score	Significance*	Type	Notes
				and new fossils are likely exposed regularly. Monitoring the fossils that erode out of this site would likely be quite important and productive, Chinle Formation, Petrified Forest Member.
42Ws234v	30	Significant	Vert	Like site 42Ws234, it should be monitored for new exposure of important fossils, Chinle Formation, Petrified Forest Member.
42Ws244t	12	Significant	Trace	Very vulnerable site that has sustained substantial damage since last visited in 2003, Kayenta Formation.
42Ws245t	40	Significant	Trace	This is another very interesting and vulnerable track site in the Kolob Canyon Area, Kayenta Formation.
42Ws247t	55	Significant	Trace	Could be easily monitored in combination with nearby sites, Kayenta Formation.
42Ws253v	60	Significant	Vert	A bone site that is located in a wash. Monitoring this site could provide better understanding of the potential for sites in washes to be covered or uncovered by sediment over time, Chinle Formation, Shinarump Member.
42Ws255t	55	Important	Trace	A large track site that is very susceptible to erosion, Kayenta Formation.
42Ws260t	30	Important	Trace	This site has suffered destruction from natural erosion which needs documentation, Moenave Formation, Whitmore Point Member.
42Ws291t	30	Significant	Trace	A large track site with casts weathering out, Kayenta Formation.
42Ws297v	45	Important	Trace	A large trackway site that is possibly susceptible to both natural and human erosion.
42Ws298t	40	Critical	Trace	A site containing very important and scientifically significant material. This is possibly the oldest Mesozoic tracksite in North America, Moenkopi Formation, Virgin Limestone Member.
42Ws340t	35	Important	Trace	This site is likely very susceptible to natural and possibly human disturbance, Moenkopi Formation, Virgin Limestone Member.
42Ws581	55	Important	Trace	Could easily be monitored in conjunction with site 42Ws260 site, Moenave Formation, Whitmore Point Member.
42Ws580	30	Important	Veg	Site located directly in an active stream so is susceptible to erosion and destruction. The site exhibits rare pyrite replacement in the petrified wood, Chinle Formation, Shinarump Conglomerate Member.
42Ws582	40	Important	Trace	This is a small block with a track that was collected in 2011 so it is deleted for monitoring, Moenave Formation, Springdale Member.

*Significance Descriptors

> **Critical**– any site producing type, very rare, or reference fossil material
> **Significant**– any site producing rare or unusually well-preserved material
> **Important**– any site producing common but abundant fossil material
> **Insignificant**– any site producing poorly preserved or less abundant but common material
> **Unimportant**– any site producing very poorly preserved and/or less abundant material

Procedures Common to all Field Activities

Field activities consist of documenting new paleontological sites and long-term monitoring of previously documented sites. In rare circumstances, where specimens are of exceptional value and/or are at great risk of being lost if left *in situ*, some specimens might be collected. Park staff should ensure that fossils are included in the park's Scope of Collections statement before making any field collections. Zion NP's Scope of Collections statement does include paleontological specimens. Collection procedures are not included in this protocol.

A job hazard analysis (JHA) will be prepared for all NPS employees and volunteers involved in field paleontological activities in the park. Most documented paleontological sites in Zion NP are located on steep rocky slopes, with poor footing and large drop-offs, and are additionally subject to severe weather. The risks involved with accessing these sites will be identified in the JHA, along with measures to mitigate the risks and respond to emergencies, and these will be reviewed with the field staff. Mitigation measures will include, at a minimum: trip planning; emergency communications; and a check-in procedure.

An Environmental Screening Form will be completed by the park physical sciences program lead to identify potential environmental impacts of inventory and monitoring activities. Park review will identify impacts and mitigation measures. This process requires 30-60 days for completion, so should be initiated well before a seasonal or volunteer paleontological staff member begins duty.

Documenting a New Paleontological Locality

Field Methods

New sites should be documented using the procedures in SOP-2. A site name and temporary site number will be assigned. A permanent site number will be requested from the Utah Geological Survey which will be the number used for future identification[1]. The Paleontological Locality Database Form (Appendix B) and Paleontological Isolated Find Data Form (Appendix D) are park-specific, but can be adapted to any park service area. For example, Grand Canyon National Park includes river miles on their forms and Glen Canyon National Recreation Area includes Lake Powell reference points such as nearest buoy number and whether sites are below high water level. Refer also to the guidelines for field notebook use outlined in SOP-5.

Park staff and visitors may observe fossils in the field and should be encouraged to report them to the appropriate staff. Visitor centers and ranger stations can have an electronic version of the Paleontological Site Report forms (Appendix F) available upon request. Park staff should assist visitors with completing the form and gathering specific location information including any photos or GPS data. Badlands National Park has used Visitor Report Forms for over ten years, resulting in the discovery of significant new sites.

Data Management

Upon return to the office, any blank fields on the documentation forms should be completed. Once the form is complete, it should be converted to digital format. If a paper form is used, it should be scanned and saved as a PDF file (at least 150 dpi resolution). If the data was entered directly into the Microsoft Word document, back-up procedures for digital data should be discussed with park's information technology staff. The data contained in the form should also be entered into the Microsoft Access site database. Zion NP currently uses a Microsoft Excel (.xls) database, but will be converting this to Microsoft Access. Microsoft Access is currently the digital database standard for the National Park Service. All electronic files must be maintained so that they are no more than two versions behind the current standard version or software. If files are inactive (i.e. site forms), they can be converted to the American Standard Code for Information Interchange (ASCII) format. All electronic files should be accompanied by "read me.txt" files explaining what the data represents, how it was gathered, any quality checks that were completed and other relevant information. See the Inventory and Monitoring network Data Management Plans for more details (http://science.nature.nps.gov/im/datamgmt/dmplans.cfm).

Original forms should be filed in separate folders for each site. Assemble site folders, which consist of a completed Paleontological Locality Database Form (Appendix B), Paleontological Locality Condition Evaluation Form (Appendix C), site notes, photographs with captions (overviews and fossil close-ups) and a map showing site location (map can be topographic, aerial, Google Earth or ArcGIS).

See additional details about data management in SOP-8.

---

[1] The Utah Geological Survey (UGS) paleontological site database is managed in consideration of the confidentiality provision for the specific location of fossils on public lands. UGS manages site data in accordance with the 1998 Omnibus Management Act and the Paleontological Resource Preservation Act (2009).

A site locality number should be requested from the Utah Geological Survey for each new site, which will replace temporary numbers in the database and file.

Personnel Requirements and Training

Documentation of new paleontological localities should be done by staff familiar with geological and paleontological field methods. Ideally, the person should have a degree in geology or biology and have completed independent paleontological research in the past. When specialized staff is unavailable, the site can be initially documented by any park staff with training in paleontological site monitoring. A note should be made for an expert to return and evaluate the site in the future.

Operational Requirements

It is unknown how many new sites will be discovered annually, and this number will be strongly influenced by the amount of field time devoted by qualified personnel. A conservative estimate would be five new sites a year, which might constitute 80 hours of labor for documentation depending on site location, extent and complexity.

Equipment required for field documentation includes:

- field notebook,

- Paleontological Locality Database Form (Appendix B),

- Paleontological Locality Condition Evaluation Form (Appendix C),

- Paleontological Isolated Find Data Form (Appendix D),

- compass,

- GPS,

- camera,

- scale bar,

- meter stick,

- sticky notes,

- writing utensils,

- hand lens,

- appropriate safety equipment (mask, hearing protection, etc.) and

- park radio.

Optional equipment includes: Trackway Worksheet (Appendix E), handheld broom, toothbrush, probe, rock hammer, Brunton compass, Mylar plastic, one meter grid, casting supplies (plaster, latex or mold putty), plastic zipper bags, and paper specimen tags. In addition, access to a computer with ArcGIS will be necessary. If any fossil specimens are collected as part of the site documentation process, these should be turned over to the park curator with all appropriate field notes, photographs, maps and other data for inclusion in the park museum collections.

Periodic Monitoring of Paleontological Sites

Field Methods

Site monitoring involves completing the Paleontological Locality Condition Evaluation Form (Appendix C). This form gives a numeric value to the condition observed at the time of the evaluation. A trend in the numeric value should be measured over time as a proxy for site health improving or deteriorating. Monitoring should be completed according to the procedures in SOP-3. While all sites may not be included in a periodic monitoring program, records of site visits should be kept for all sites. During these visits, recommendations should be made for when the next monitoring visit should occur. Refer also to the guidelines for field notebook use outlined in SOP-5.

Data Management

Upon return to the office, any blank fields on the monitoring forms should be completed. It may be helpful to review additional photos to identify any changes in condition. Once the form is complete, it should be converted to digital format. If a paper form is used, it should be scanned and saved as a PDF file (at least 150 dpi resolution). If the data was entered directly into the Microsoft Word document, back-up procedures for digital data should be discussed with park's information technology staff. The data contained in the form should also be entered into the Microsoft Access site database. Microsoft Access is currently the digital database standard for the National Park Service. All electronic files must be maintained so that they are no more than two versions behind the current standard version or software. If files are inactive (i.e. site forms), they can be converted to the American Standard Code for Information Interchange (ASCII) format. All electronic files should be accompanied by "read me.txt" files explaining what the data represents, how it was gathered, any quality checks that were completed and other relevant information. See the Inventory and Monitoring network Data Management Plans for more details (http://science.nature.nps.gov/im/datamgmt/dmplans.cfm).

Original forms, in both paper and electronic formats, should be filed in the appropriate site folder. Paleontological site information is considered sensitive and should not be shared with the general public. Section 207 of the National Parks Omnibus Management Act of 1998 (1998 Omnibus Act) authorizes the NPS to withhold information concerning the nature and specific location of paleontological resources from the public in response to a Freedom of Information Act request, unless the Secretary determines that (1) disclosure of the information would further the purposes of the unit of the National Park System in which the resource or object is located and would not create an unreasonable risk of harm, theft, or destruction of the resource or object, including individual organic or inorganic specimens and (2) disclosure is consistent with other applicable laws protecting the resource or object. Make a copy of the monitoring form and add it to the field version of the site file. See additional details about data management in SOP-8.

Personnel Requirements and Training

Monitoring of paleontological localities should be done by staff familiar with paleontological site monitoring techniques. Subject-matter experts can train interested staff to monitor sites. Training should provide appropriate site files, describe the pertinent forms and include hands-on training at a site. It is valuable for Visitor & Resource Protection (V&RP) staff to be aware of paleontological localities located near visitor use areas. V&RP staff can monitor visitor use and avoid sensitive areas when responding to incidents. Assisting with site monitoring will also familiarize rangers with the appearance of local fossils and prepare them to respond to any incidents of fossil damage or theft.

If non-specialists observe damage or discover new fossils during site monitoring, they should contact the park's paleontology lead immediately. The paleontology program lead can conduct a follow-up visit, determine if management actions are necessary and/or contact local paleontologists for an evaluation.

Operational Requirements

Zion NP has chosen 21 paleontological resource localities (sites) for periodic monitoring. These 21 sites were selected based on the availability of locality data, presence inside the park boundary, mitigation ranking from DeBlieux (2005), susceptibility to natural and human-caused erosion, fossil significance, accessibility, and proximity to other sites. For additional explanation of why these criteria were used, see Markle (2008). Given the location of these sites, and time needed to become familiar with local fossils, a monitoring site visit to all 21 sites is likely to require approximately two months of field and office work.

Equipment required for field documentation includes:

- copies of existing site descriptions including maps and photographs,

- field notebook,

- Paleontological Locality Database Form (Appendix B),

- Paleontological Locality Condition Evaluation Form (Appendix C),

- Paleontological Isolated Find Data Form (Appendix D),

- compass,

- GPS,

- camera,

- scale bar,

- meter stick,

- sticky notes,

- writing utensils,

- hand lens and

- appropriate safety equipment (mask, hearing protection, etc.).

Optional equipment includes: Trackway Worksheet (Appendix E), handheld broom, toothbrush, probe, rock hammer, Brunton compass, Mylar plastic, one meter grid, casting supplies (plaster, latex or mold putty), plastic zipper bags, and paper specimen tags. In addition, access to a computer with ArcGIS will be necessary.

Long-Term Paleontological Site Monitoring Techniques

Repeat Photography

Repeat photography is a powerful tool for monitoring. Photo points must be established for large-scale and small-scale repeat photography, where consistent points of reference and perspectives are available over time (Santucci et al. 2009). Establishing a photo point requires a detailed written description of its location and visible landmarks. It may be helpful to have GPS coordinates for the photo point and azimuth directions. Using the written description and printed copies of previous photographs, the camera location should be matched. Under special circumstances, photo points can be marked using a permanent marker such as a rebar stake. This was done at the National Park Service prototype monitoring site GLCA 1 (Figure 2). This marker serves as a geo-reference point and photo point for repeat photography (Kirkland et al. 2010). See further information in SOP-2, SOP-3 and SOP-6.

Figure 2. Rebar stake placed as a permanent locator at National Park Service prototype monitoring site (GLCA 1). Stakes are not necessary for repeat photography.

Repeat photography can be completed by a trained volunteer in a few hours' time, does not require specialized equipment and has a minimal cost. Repeat photography and documents will eventually be archival records and as such fall under the jurisdiction of museum management. Arrangements should be made with the park curator for accessioning and archiving all data related to paleontological resource monitoring, and to develop finding aids to facilitate park staff finding this data in the archives.

Erosion Stakes

Multiple erosion stakes of galvanized steel can be installed in a rock unit to measure natural erosion rates (Santucci et al. 2009). The stakes should be installed perpendicular to the surface, with the baseline level marked directly on the stake at the point where it enters the ground surface. During subsequent visits, any changes in the ground surface level relative to the stake should be recorded. For the first five years after installation, monitoring should take place at least annually. Installation of stakes is best performed by a trained geologist or paleontologist, but monitoring can be completed by a trained volunteer.

Photogrammetry can also be used for long-term monitoring of erosion rates. See SOP-6 for additional information.

Crack Monitors

Crack monitors can be used to monitor the expansion of natural joints in fossil-bearing rock layers (Figure 3). Commercial crack monitors are commonly used to measure cracks in masonry structures (Fisher 2008). Crack monitors consist of two overlapping plates that are attached with epoxy on either side of a crack or joint. Epoxy generally provides permanent attachment, although vandalism has been observed in Glen Canyon National Recreation Area (Figure 4). As an alternative, joint expansion can be measured by permanently marking either side of a joint and using calipers to measure the distance in between. Joint expansion observed should be documented in photographs, which can be taken by trained volunteers.

Figure 3. Crack monitors (circled) installed across a natural joint in Glen Canyon National Recreation Area (GLCA 10). The rock on the left side of the joint is hollow, and there is concern that it may detach. These crack monitors were placed out of easy reach of visitors to reduce the potential for vandalism.

Figure 4. Crack monitor displaced by vandalism at Glen Canyon National Recreation Area in September 2011 (GLCA 1).

Climatic Records

Climatic records including temperature and precipitation should be compiled for at least a five-year period (Santucci et al. 2009). An average freeze-thaw index can be calculated using this data (see Santucci et al. 2009 for methods). Fossil sites in areas of high annual precipitation or with a high freeze-thaw index require more frequent monitoring. During periods of increased precipitation, additional monitoring visits may be warranted. Long-term climate records exist for Zion Canyon, St. George and Cedar City. Shorter records exist for Dalton Wash, Cave Valley and Kolob Canyons.

Geohazard Monitoring

Potentially catastrophic geohazards that could affect fossil sites should be identified. This can be accomplished by a thorough review of local processes, relevant geologic maps and scientific literature as well as consulting with professional geologists (Santucci et al. 2009). Geological hazard maps and a risk assessment exists for Zion NP (Lund et. al. 2010). When necessary, specialized equipment such as seismometers, GPS stations or ground motion sensors can be installed. Photogrammetric methods can also be used. In Zion NP, the area of the park with the greatest risk of seismic activity is the Kolob Canyons area, which is bisected by the Hurricane Fault that has a history of Quaternary surface rupturing events. For that reason, fossils on the underside of overhanging ledges in this area are particularly prone to rockfall so such sites are candidates for frequent monitoring, or collection. Because the Hurricane Fault is capable of producing quakes with a magnitude of 6.6 to 7.3, and other less active faults are present in the vicinity, the entire park can be considered seismically active.

Technology-Enhanced Monitoring and Digital Mapping

Digital elevation data and geospatial data for paleontological localities can be used to create maps showing areas of high-, medium- and low slopes (Santucci et al. 2009). This assessment will help identify the best locations for installation of erosion stakes. A landslide assessment could be completed based on aerial photos. In shoreline environments, tidal gauges or flow meters could be installed to record changes in water depth and velocity. Photographic or video surveillance could be employed at sites experiencing high visitor use levels. GIS maps can be produced that overlay geohazard data or shoreline data with fossil localities. This may help identify sites at an elevated level of risk of damage due to natural processes. These techniques are relatively expensive and require significant staff expertise.

Prioritizing Paleontological Sites for Monitoring

If a list of known paleontological sites is provided, it is important to prioritize which sites should be monitored and how often. Refer to the procedure outlined in SOP-4.

The Utah Geologic Survey uses a scale to determine the scientific significance of sites that ranges from Critical- to Unimportant (DeBlieux et al. 2005). Critical and Significant sites, at a minimum, should be considered for monitoring.

Category	Description
Critical	Any site producing type, very rare or reference fossil material
Significant	Any site producing rare or unusually well-preserved material
Important	Any site producing common but abundant fossil material
Insignificant	Any site producing poorly preserved or less abundant but common material
Unimportant	Any site producing very poorly preserved and/or less abundant material

Markle (2008) recommends 21 paleontological sites at Zion NP for long-term monitoring, based on the availability of locality data, presence inside the park boundary, mitigation ranking from DeBlieux (2005), susceptibility to natural and human-caused erosion, fossil significance, accessibility, and proximity to other sites. The selected sites include a variety of fossil types located throughout Zion NP. Fourteen of these sites were recommended for monitoring based on their poor monitoring score. Seven sites recommended for monitoring were in fair condition based on their score. Many of the seven sites in fair condition were also recommended based on the presence of significant fossils.

Data Management
A database should be created to store all site data in one location. Currently, this is a Microsoft Excel file (.xls). In the future this will be converted to a Microsoft Access database. For more details about databases, see SOP-8. All original paper records, photographs, maps, stratigraphic sections and other data should be placed in the park museum archives. There should be a regular schedule for the transfer of these records to the park curator.

Personnel Requirements and Training
Prioritization of paleontological site monitoring should be performed by a trained geologist or paleontologist. The person should also be familiar with managing natural resources on public lands, and ideally had experience monitoring natural resources in the field.

Operational Requirements
If the park does not have a database, one can be created based on site forms, field notes, trip reports, paleontological literature, and museum collection records. Depending on the park's size, this effort could require anywhere from a few weeks to a few months. The National Park Service standard for databases is Microsoft Access, which should be utilized for any new databases.

Literature Cited

Baker, T. and B. Shaw. 2012. Technical guidelines and standard operating procedures: Digital photograph management strategy for the monitoring and maintenance program, Glen Canyon National Recreation Area, 18 p. On file at GLCA.

Biek, R.F., G. C. Willis, M. D. Hylland and H.H. Doelling. 2003. Geology of Zion National Park, Utah in Sprinkel, D. A., T. C. Chidsey, Jr., and P. B. Anderson, editors. Geology of Utah's parks and monuments (2nd edition). Utah Geological Association and Bryce Canyon Natural History Association Publication, v. 28, p. 107-137.

Biek, R. F., G. C. Willis, M. D. Hylland, and H. H. Doelling. 2010. Geology of Zion National Park, Utah. Pages 109-143 *in* Sprinkel, D. A., T. C. Chidsey, Jr., and P. B. Anderson, editors. Geology of Utah's parks and monuments (3rd edition). Utah Geological Association, Salt Lake City, UT. Publication 28.

DeBlieux, D. D., J. A. Smith, J. L. McGuire, J. I. Kirkland, and V. L. Santucci. 2005. Zion National Park paleontological survey. Technical Information Center (TIC) # D-177.

DeBlieux, D. D., J. I. Kirkland, J. A. Smith, J. McGuire, and V. L. Santucci. 2006. An overview of the paleontology of Upper Triassic and Lower Jurassic rocks in Zion National Park, Utah. Pages 490-501 *in* Harris, J. D., S. G. Lucas, J. A. Spielmann, M. G. Lockley, A. R. C. Milner, and J. I. Kirkland, editors. The Triassic-Jurassic terrestrial transition. New Mexico Museum of Natural History and Science, Albuquerque, NM. Bulletin 37. Online. http://ib.berkeley.edu/labs/barnosky/DeBlieux_et_al_%28Zion_Park%29.pdf. Accessed May 2012.

Falkingham, P. L. 2012. Acquisition of high resolution three-dimensional models using free, open-source, photogrammetric software. Palaeontologia Electronica 15(1):1--15.

Fisher, P. 2008. Appendix F: Management and monitoring: structural evaluation guideline *in* Preservation and Management Guidelines for Vanishing Treasures Resources by J. M. Barrow, Intermountain Region, National Park Service, United States Department of the Interior.

Fremd, T. 1992. Paleontological resource management, NPS-77, and its practical applications. Proceedings of the Third Conference on Fossil Resources, Programs with Abstracts, National Park Service Technical Report NPS/NRFOBU/NRR-94-14, p. 18.

Hamblin, A. H., M. G. Lockley, and A. R. C. Milner. 2006. More reports of theropod dinosaur tracksites from the Kayenta Formation (Lower Jurassic), Washington County, Utah: implications for describing the Springdale megatracksite. Pages 276-281 *in* Harris, J. D., S. G. Lucas, J. A. Spielmann, M. G. Lockley, A. R. C. Milner, and J. I. Kirkland, editors. The Triassic-Jurassic terrestrial transition. New Mexico Museum of Natural History and Science, Albuquerque, NM. Bulletin 37.

Kirkland, J. K., S. K. Madsen, J. B. Ehler, D. D. DeBlieux, L. Weaver and V. Santucci. 2010. Final report for paleontological resources inventory and monitoring at Glen Canyon National Recreation Area, 165 p. On file at GLCA.

Long, J. D. and B. R. Mitchell. 2012. Northeast Temperate Network Long-Term Rocky Mountain Intertidal Monitoring Protocol. Natural Resource Report. NPS/NETN/NRR— 2012/495. National Park Service, Fort Collins, Colorado.

Lucas, S. G. and L. H. Tanner. 2006. The Springdale Member of the Kayenta Formation, Lower Jurassic of Utah-Arizona. Pages 71-76 in Harris, J. D., S. G. Lucas, J. A. Spielmann, M. G. Lockley, A. R. C. Milner, and J. I. Kirkland, editors. The Triassic-Jurassic terrestrial transition. New Mexico Museum of Natural History and Science, Albuquerque, NM. Bulletin 37.

Lucas, S. G., A. B. Heckert, and L. H. Tanner. 2005. Arizona's Jurassic fossil vertebrates and the age of the Glen Canyon Group. Pages 95-104 in Heckert, A. B. and S. G. Lucas, editors. Vertebrate paleontology in Arizona. New Mexico Museum of Natural History and Science, Albuquerque, NM. Bulletin 29.

Lund, William R,. Tyler R. Knudsen, and David L. Sharrow, 2010. Geologic Hazards of the Zion National Park Geologic-Hazard Study Area, Washington and Kane Counties, Utah. Utah Geological Survey, Special Study 133. Salt Lake City, Utah. ISBN 978-1-55791-833-8

Markle, B. R. 2008. Development of Paleontological Resource Monitoring Program, Zion National Park. National Park Service, Fort Collins, CO.

Mickelson, D. L., A. R. C. Milner, D. D. DeBlieux, and J. L. McGuire. 2006. The oldest known Early Triassic fossil vertebrate footprints in North America, from Zion National Park, Utah. Pages 141-144 in Lucas, S. G., J. A. Spielmann, P. M. Hester, J. P. Kenworthy, and V. L. Santucci, editors. America's antiquities: 100 years of managing fossils on federal lands. New Mexico Museum of Natural History and Science, Albuquerque, NM. Bulletin 34.

Milner, A. R. C. and S. Z. Spears, leaders. 2007. Mesozoic and Cenozoic paleoichnology of southwestern Utah. In Lund, W. R., editor. Field guide to geologic excursions in southern Utah. Utah Geological Association, Salt Lake City, UT. Publication 35.

National Park Service. 2009. Geologic Resources Division: Paleontology Program Action Plan, Draft version.

National Park Service. 2011. Field data collection using global positioning systems: Standard operating procedures and guidelines. National Park Service: Resource Information Services Division.

Oakley, K. L., L. P. Thomas and S. G. Fancy. 2003. Guidelines for long-term monitoring protocols. Wildlife Society Bulletin 31(4): 1000-1003.

Santucci, V. L. and J. I. Kirkland. 2010. An overview of National Park Service paleontological resources from the Parks and Monuments in Utah. Pages 589-623 in Sprinkel, D. A., T. C.

Chidsey, Jr., and P. B. Anderson, editors. Geology of Utah's parks and monuments (3rd edition). Utah Geological Association, Salt Lake City, UT. Publication 28. Online. http://ugs.academia.edu/JamesKirkland/Papers/190514/Santucci_V._L._and_Kirkland_J._I._2010_An_Overview_of_National_Park_Service_Paleontological_Resources_from_the_Parks_and_Monuments_in_Utah_in_D.A._Sprinkel_T.C._Chidsey_Jr._and_P.B._Anderson_eds._Geology_of_Utahs_Parks_and_Monuments_Utah_Geological_Association_Publication_28_third_edition_._p._589-623. Accessed May 2012.

Santucci, V. L., J. P. Kenworthy, and A. L. Mims. 2009. Monitoring in situ paleontological resources. Pages 189-204 *in* Young, R. and L. Norby, editors. Geological monitoring. Geological Society of America, Boulder, CO.

Stewart, J. H., F. G. Poole, and R. F. Wilson. 1972. Stratigraphy and origin of the Chinle Formation and related Upper Triassic strata in the Colorado Plateau region. U.S. Geological Survey, Reston, VA. Professional Paper 690.

Tweet, J.S., V.L. Santucci, T. Connors and J.P. Kenworthy. 2012 Paleontologial Resource Inventory and Monitoring: Northern Colorado Plateau Network. Natural Resource Technical Report NPS/NCPN/NRTR—2012/585. National Park Service, Fort Collins, Colorado.

Willis, G. C. and R. F. Biek. 2001. Quaternary incision rates of the Colorado River and major tributaries in the Colorado Plateau. Pages 119-123 *in* Young, R. A. and E. E. Spamer, editors. Colorado River origin and evolution: proceedings of the symposium held at Grand Canyon National Park in June 2000. Grand Canyon Association, Grand Canyon, AZ. Monograph 12.

Appendix A
Statutory Authorities for the Management and Protection of National Park Service Paleontological Resources and Values

The NPS has a variety of legal, regulatory and policy authorities which directly or indirectly relate to the management of paleontological resources. A list of the key statutes is presented below (NPS, 2009).

- Antiquities Act of 1906: (16 U.S.C. 431-433, 34 Stat. 225)

- National Park Service Organic Act: (16 U.S.C. 1 et seq., 39 Stat. 535)

- Wilderness Act of 1964: (16 U.S.C. 1131 et seq., 78 Stat 890, P.L. 88-577)

- National Environmental Policy Act: (42 U.S.C. 4321 et seq., 83 Stat 852, P.L. 91-190)

- Archeological Resource Protection Act of 1979: (16 U.S.C. 470aa, 93 Stat. 721, P.L. 96-95).

- Alaska National Interest Lands Conservation Act of 1980: (16 U.S.C. 3101 et seq., 94 Stat 2371, P.L. 96-487)

- Federal Cave Resources Protection Act of 1988 (102 Stat, 4546, P.L. 100-691)

- 1998 National Park Service Omnibus Management Act

- Consolidated Natural Resources Act of 2008

- Paleontological Resource Preservation Act (2009): (P.L. 111-11)

- Park System Resource Protection Act (19jj)

- Other relevant statutes include the National Trails System Act of 1968, the Wild and Scenic Rivers Act of 1968, and the Land and Water Conservation Fund Program Act of 1965.

Appendix B
Paleontological Locality Database Form

ZION NATIONAL PARK
PALEONTOLOGICAL LOCALITY DATABASE FORM

FORM DATA

Form Filled Out By:	**Form Date:**
Record Entered Into the Database By:	**Date Record Entered:**

LOCALITY DATA

Locality Number: _____	**Other Locality Numbers/Field #:**
Locality Name:	

Locality Type: ☐ *Vertebrate*, ☐ *Invertebrate*, ☐ *Plant*, ☐ *Ichnoform (Track)* , ☐ *Other:* _____

State: *Utah*	**County:** ☐ *Kane,* ☐ *Iron,* ☐ *Washington*

Law Enforcement District: ☐ Canyon, ☐ Plateau, ☐ Kolob Canyons ☐Wilderness? ☐ Inholding?

USGS 7.5' Quadrangle: _____

Legals: T._____South, R. _____West, Sec _____, _____¼ , _____¼ , _____¼

Locality Description:

UTMs 12s	**Easting:** _____	**Northing:** _____
Datum: ☐*NAD83* ☐*WGS84* ☐*NAD27*☐*Unknown*		**Field Accuracy:**
Latitude: _____/_____/_____		**Longitude:** _____/_____/_____
or Decimal Degrees: _____		or Decimal Degrees: _____
Elevation: _____		**Areal Extant (mxm):** ☐<1 ☐1-5 ☐>5

LITHOLOGY AND PALEONTOLOGICAL RESOURCE DESCRIPTIONS

Geologic Formation: ☐ *Kaibab,* ☐ *Moenkopi,* ☐ *Chinle,* ☐ *Moenave,* ☐ *Kayenta(incl. Springdale),* ☐ *Navajo,*☐ *Temple Cap,* ☐ *Carmel,* ☐ *Cedar Mountain,* ☐ *Dakota,* ☐ *Volcanic Flows,* ☐ *Surface/Quaternary*

Member/Series/Facies: _____ ☐*unknown*

Vertical Position: _____ (+/-) meters above/below contact or marker bed

Lithology/Substrate: ☐*ash,* ☐*limestone,* ☐*mudstone,* ☐*sandstone,* ☐*shale,* ☐*siltstone,* ☐*clay,* ☐*mud,* ☐*sand,* ☐*conglomerate,* ☐*soil*

Depositional Environment: ☐*aeolian,* ☐*fluvial,* ☐*lacustrine,* ☐*marine,* ☐*other,* ☐*unknown*

Lithologic Description:

Period: □*Permian*, □*Triassic*, □*Jurassic*, □*Cretaceous*, □*Tertiary*, □*Pleistocene*, □*Holocene*	
Strike and Dip of Deposits: Strike_____ Dip _____ □ *unknown*	
Taxa Present: □*Mammals*, □*Reptiles*, □*Amphibians*, □*Aves*, □*Fish*, □*Plants*, □*Ichnofossils*, □*Invertebrates*	
Dominant Taxa: (in order of relative abundance) 1. 2. 3.	**Specimens Collected:** □*yes* □*no* □*unknown* *Type:* □*Float* □*In situ (Local concentrations? Dispersed?)* □*both*

CONDITION AND DISTURBANCE

Site Permanently Marked for Relocation: , □*yes*, □*no* Marker Type/Description _____	**Long-term Monitoring Site:** , □*yes*, □*no*, □*unknown*
Site Condition: □*pristine*, □*fragmented*, □*scattered*	**Poached:** , □*yes*, □*no* , □*unknown*
Anthropogenic Factors: □*trail*, □*road*, □*campground*, □*trampling*, □*vandalism*, □*theft* *(in near vicinity or that have occurred)*	
Erosion Type: , □*no erosion*, □*slope movement*, □*storm water*, □*chemical weathering* , □*unknown*, □*lake erosion*, □*spalling*, □*physical weathering (wind/rain)*	
Erosion Significance: □*Nominal* (minor or not affecting paleontological resources) □*Moderate* (likely to affect paleontological resources in the future) □*Major* (damage or loss of paleontological resources occurring)	Cause of Erosion: □Natural □Exacerbated by human activities Explain: _____

Photograph Numbers:
 	
                  Photographer _____
 	
               Date Photographed _____
 	
 Additional Comments on Photographs:	

CURATORIAL/COLLECTION DATA

Permit Numbers:	
Field Numbers of Collected Specimens:	
Collected by:_____ **Date:** _____ **Repository:**_____	
Curated Specimens:	
Site Found By:	**Discovery Date:**

SITE SKETCHES, PHOTOGRAPHS AND ADDITIONAL COMMENTS

Scale:

Appendix C
Paleontological Locality Condition Evaluation Form

ZION NATIONAL PARK
PALEONTOLOGICALLOCALITY CONDITION EVALUATION FORM

Site Number: _____

Total Score

☐ **Recorded by:** _____   **Date:** ____/____/____

Last visited by:_____   **Date:** ____/____/____

Each paleontological locality will have a maximum score of 170 points. The higher the score, the better the condition of the locality. Each criterion has several selections to choose from. Please make one selection for each criterion and place its corresponding numerical score in the box. Localities with a total score higher than 90 are considered to be in good condition. Localities with a total score between 50 and 90 are marginal and some management action may be warranted. Localities with a total score of less than 50 are considered to be in poor condition and management activities need to be increased to improve the condition of the site.

#1. DISTURBANCE
The present condition of the site is evaluated in terms of the degree of human disturbance or abuse that is threatening or destroying the integrity of the locality. Examples include: greater than normal rates of erosion resulting from human activity, illegal removal of fossils from the locality.

☐ *Poor condition* – the locality is being rapidly eroded or there are high levels of illegal removal of fossils (0 points).

☐ *Moderate condition* – a slight increase of erosion above normal levels, occasional removal of fossils illegally (10 points).

☐ *Outstanding condition* – erosion and exposure of locality is within normal rates for the area, no evidence of illegal collecting or removal of fossils (20 points).

MITIGATION:

☐ *No action (0 points)*

☐ *Cause of erosion due to human activity has been stopped, increase in monitoring by resource managers or law enforcement has reduced illegal removal of fossils (15 points)*

Total Disturbance Points (condition + mitigation): ☐

#2. FRAGILITY

The locality is evaluated according to its ability to withstand damage. The vulnerability of a locality depends on the type of sediments that contain the fossil and their resistance to erosion, local rates of natural processes that cause erosion (i.e. rainfall, wind and lake action), and the degree of exposure of a locality to these natural processes.

    □ *High fragility* – the lithology of the locality is unconsolidated and easily eroded, fossils are exposed on a seasonal basis. In Zion NP this would include fossils found on the underside of overhanging ledges (0 points).

    □ *Moderate fragility* – the erosion of the locality and exposure of the fossils takes longer than a single season but occurs within a few years (10 points).

    □ *Low fragility* – the lithology of the locality does not erode quickly, fossils are exposed at a low rate and the locality is not modified except over long periods of time (20 points).

MITIGATION:

    □ *No action (0 points)*

    □ *Fossils are collected and documented on a regular basis as part of cyclic monitoring in order to prevent loss (15 points)*

Total Fragility Points (fragility + mitigation):

#3. POTENTIAL FOR THEFT OR DAMAGE OF FOSSILS

    □ *Highly attractive*– fossils occur in large numbers whether of a single species or multiple species, highly concentrated in a relatively small area and easily spotted and recognized, are attractive as collectors' items, and are easily removed (0 points).

    □ *Moderately attractive* – fossils are present and recognizable but in relatively low numbers and are distributed over a larger area and may not be easily spotted and recognized, are moderately attractive to collectors, and are somewhat difficult to remove (10 points).

    □ *Low attractiveness* – fossils occur sporadically, or as single individual specimens, are not easily spotted and recognized except by professionals, are unattractive to collectors and are difficult to remove (20 points).

ACTUAL LOSS:

    □ *Significant and noticeable disappearance of fossils from area on a seasonal basis (0 points)*

☐ *Number of fossils in area is reduced by a small amount on a yearly basis (10 points)*

☐ *Number of fossils in area does not change significantly from year to year (20 points)*

MITIGATION:
☐ *No action (0 points)*

☐ *Fossils are monitored on a regular basis in order to determine if they are being lost or destroyed (10 points)*

☐ *Fossils are collected and documented on a regular basis in order to prevent loss (20 points)*

Total Abundance Points (abundance + actual loss + mitigation):

#4. ACCESS TO SITE

☐ *Easy* – site is close to roads, trails, rivers or is located in easily traversed terrain (0 points).

☐ *Moderate* – site is not close to roads, trails, rivers and site is in a location that is relatively inaccessible or not likely to be visited (10 points).

☐ *Difficult* – site is located in back country, not easily accessible and difficult to locate (20 points).

MITIGATION:
☐ *No action (0 points)*

☐ *Site is monitored by park staff (5 points)*

☐ *Actively patrolled or collected on occasion as needed (10 points)*

☐ *Site is protected by a physical barrier or structure (10 points)*

☐ *Active law enforcement protection, either visitation, surveillance or ongoing collection by researchers (20 points)*

☐ *The locality has been evaluated and is included in an established program of cyclic monitoring (10 points)*

Total Access Points (access + mitigation):

TOTAL SCORE FOR PALEONTOLOGICAL LOCALITY CONDITION:
Total Score (Total Disturbance Points +
Total Fragility Points + Total Abundance Points + Total Access Points)

PHOTOGRAPHS FOR THE LOCALITY

Photograph Name PhotographerName_SiteNumber_YYYYMMDD_PhotoID	Northing	Easting	Azimuth

ADDITIONAL COMMENTS

_____

_____

_____

_____

_____

_____

Appendix D
Paleontological Isolated Find Data Form

ZION NATIONAL PARK
PALEONTOLOGICAL ISOLATED FIND DATA FORM

Form Filled Out By:	Date:

LOCALITY DATA

State: *Utah*	County: ☐ *Kane*, ☐ *Iron*, ☐ *Washington*
USGS 7.5' Quadrangle:	**Canyon/Waterway:**

Legals: T._____South, R. _____West, Sec _____, ___¼, _____¼, _____¼

Locality Description:

UTMs 12s Easting: _____	**Northing:** _____
Datum: ☐*NAD83* ☐*WGS84* ☐*NAD27* ☐*Unknown*	**Field Accuracy:**
Latitude: _____/_____/ _____	**Longitude:** _____/_____/ _____
or Decimal Degrees: _____	or Decimal Degrees: _____
Elevation: _____	**Areal Extant (m$_x$m):** ☐<1 ☐1-5 ☐>5

LITHOLOGY AND PALEONTOLOGICAL DESCRIPTIONS

Supposed Geologic Formation: ☐ *Kaibab*, ☐ *Moenkopi*, ☐ *Chinle*, ☐ *Moenave*, ☐ *Kayenta*(incl. Springdale), ☐ *Navajo*, ☐ *Temple Cap*, ☐ *Carmel*, ☐ *Cedar Mountain*, ☐ *Dakota*, ☐ *Volcanic Flows*, ☐ *Surface/Quaternary*

Lithology/Substrate: ☐*ash*, ☐*limestone*, ☐*mudstone*, ☐*sandstone*, ☐*shale*, ☐*siltstone*, ☐*clay*, ☐*mud*, ☐*sand*, ☐*conglomerate*, ☐*soil*

Taxa Present: ☐*Mammals*, ☐*Reptiles*, ☐*Amphibians*, ☐*Aves*, ☐*Fish*, ☐*Plants*, ☐*Ichnofossils*, ☐*Invertebrates*

Specific Taxon (if known):	**Specimen Collected:** *yes* *no*

PHOTOGRAPHS:

SKETCHES AND ADDITIONAL COMMENTS

Scale:

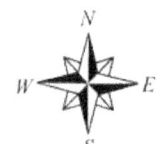

Appendix E
Trackway Worksheet

ZION NATIONAL PARK
TRACKWAY WORKSHEET
FORM DATA

Form Filled Out By:	Form Date:
Record Entered Into the Database By:	Date Record Entered:

LOCALITY DATA

Locality Number: _____	Other Locality Numbers/Field #:
Locality Name:	
Trackway Location:	

TRACKWAY DATA

Type of Track:	Total Number of Tracks:
Trackway Length:	Trackway Width:

INDIVIDUAL TRACK MEASUREMENTS (BIPEDAL OR QUADRUPEDAL) SHOULD BE ENTERED ON ATTACHED SHEETS.

(Worksheets provided by Andrew Milner, St. George Dinosaur Discovery Site at Johnson Farm.)

Bipedal Track Meristics:

Field # = number assigned to track on map

Name = Ichnotaxa (e.g. *Grallator*, *Eubrontes*, unidentified, etc)

T = total length of phalangeal part of foot skeleton

II = phalangeal length of digit II

III = phalangeal length of digit III

IV = phalangeal length of digit IV

II-IV< = divarication angle of digits II-IV

II-III < = divarication angle of digits II-III

III-IV < = divarication angle of digits III-IV

R = length of rear of phalangeal part of foot

TL = total track length

TW = total track width

TD = greatest track depth

cl = claw length

cw = proximal claw width

Bipedal Trackway Meristics:

Field # = number assigned to track on map

Name = Ichnotaxa (e.g. *Grallator*, *Eubrontes*, unidentified, etc)

TWL = total trackway length

TWW = total trackway width

Pace 1, 2, 3 etc. = distance from midpoints of right to left, and left to right tracks. Also called Step.

Stride 1, 2 etc. = distance from midpoints of right to next right, or left to next left tracks.

PA1, 2, etc. = pace or step angulation

Orient. = trackway orientation, or direction animal was traveling in.

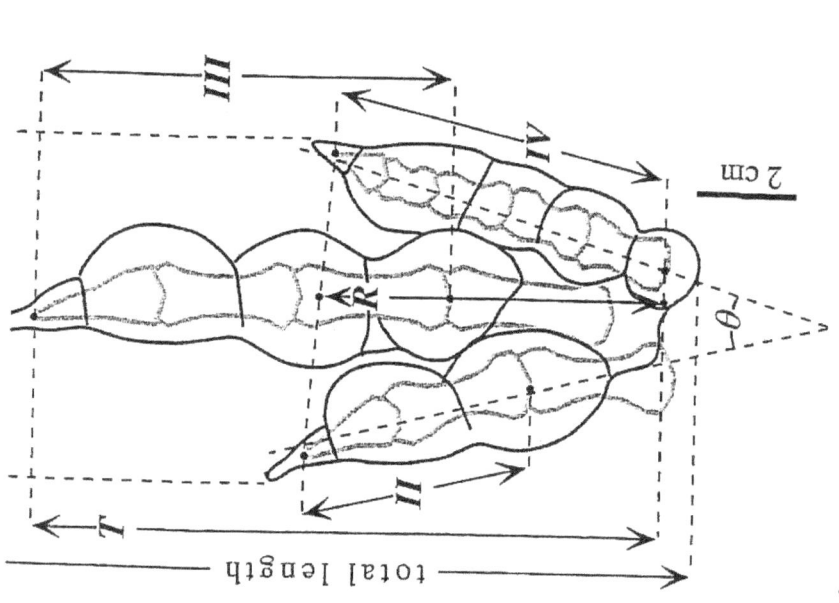

FIGURE 3. Conventions of footprint and skeletal measurements used in this paper shown on Lull's (1953) drawing of his concept of *Anchisauripus sillimani* (AC 9/14) (adapted from Farlow and Lockley (1993) and Leonardi (1987)). Measurements are: T = total length of phalangeal part of foot skeleton; R = length of rear of phalangeal part of foot; R' = R * [1/cos (q / 2)] = corrected θ = divarication angle of digits II-IV; R' = R * [1/cos (q / 2)] = corrected

From: Andrew Milner, St. George Dinosaur Site

BIPEDAL DINOSAUR TRACKWAY MEASURMENTS

LOCALITY:

STRAT.:

FIELD #:

DATE:

RECORDER:

FIELD #	NAME; T#	TWL	TWW	Pace 1	Pace 2	Pace 3	Pace 4	Stride 1	Stride 2	PA1	PA2	Orient.

Quadrupedal Track Meristics:

Field # = number assigned to track on map
Trackway Name = Ichnotaxa
MTL = total manus track length
MTW = total manus track width
MTD = greatest manus track depth
PTL = total pes track length
PTW = total pes track width
PTD = greatest pes track depth
<PRM = angle of pes rotation from midline of trackway
MI-OT< = manus inner to outer digit divarication angle
PI-OT< = pes inner to outer digit divarication angle
M-orient. = manus orientation
P-orient. = pes orientation

Quadrupedal Trackway Meristics:

Field # = number assigned to track on map

Trackway Name = Ichnotaxa (e.g. *Grallator*
TWL = total trackway length
TWW = total trackway width

MPace 1, 2 etc. = distance from midpoints of right to left manus, and left to right manus tracks.
PPace 1, 2 etc. = distance from midpoints of right to left pes, and left to right pes tracks.
MStride 1, 2 etc. = distance from midpoints of right to next right manus, or left to next left manus tracks.
PStride 1, 2 etc. = distance from midpoints of right to next right pes, or left to next left pes tracks.
MPA1, 2, etc. = manus pace or step angulation
PPA1, 2, etc. = pes pace or step angulation
Orient. = trackway orientation, or direction animal was traveling in.

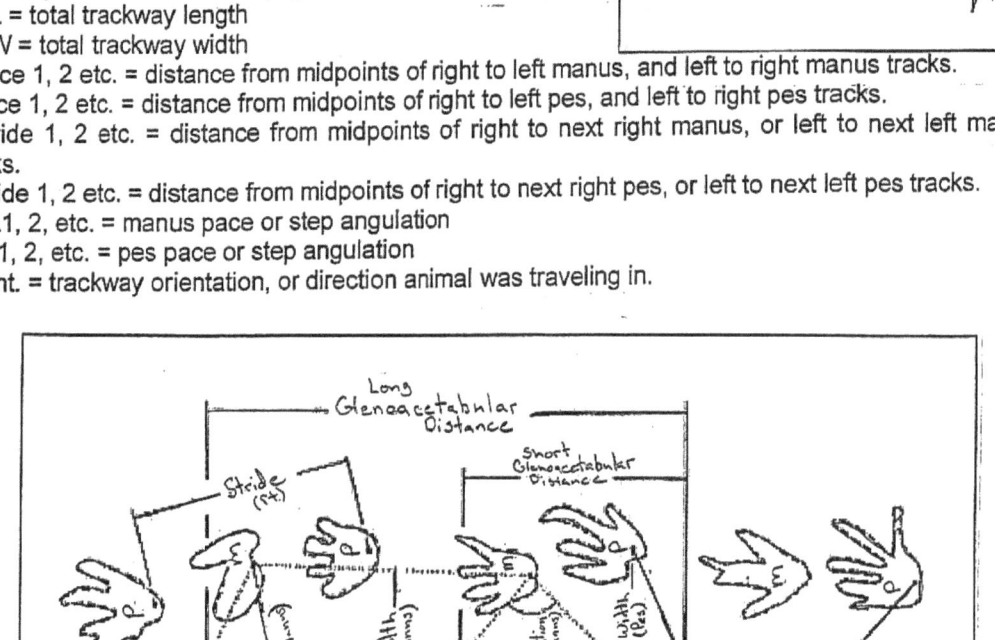

QUADRUPEDAL TRACK MEASURMENTS

LOCALITY: _____

STRAT.: _____

FIELD #: _____

DATE: _____

RECORDER: _____

FIELD #	NAME; T#; L-R	MTL	MTW	MTD	PTL	PTW	PTD	<PRM	MI-OT<	PI-OT<	M-orient.	P-orient.

TRACKWAY SKETCH AND ADDITIONAL COMMENTS

Scale:

Appendix F
Paleontological Site Report

Date Observed _____
Ranger Station/Visitor Center_____
Employee Name_____   .

PALEONTOLOGICAL SITE REPORT: VISITOR FIELD ID

DESCRIPTION OF SITE LOCATION: HELP US LOCATE THE FOSSIL EASILY BY ANSWERING ALL
QUESTIONS. INCLUDE ANY ADDITIONAL INFORMATION YOU FEEL WOULD BE OF ASSISTANCE. PLEASE
MARK THE LOCATION OF THE FOSSIL ON THE MAP.

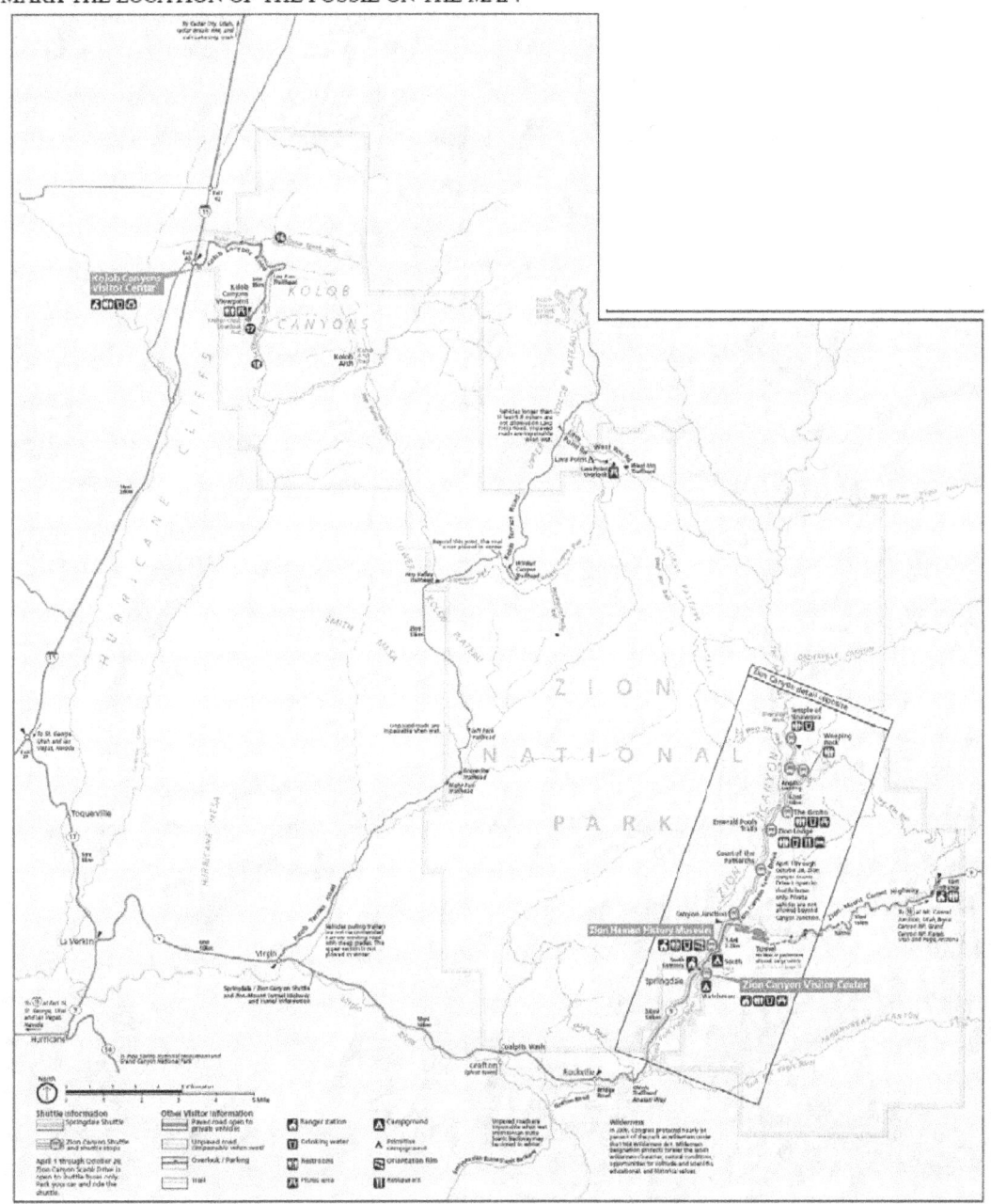

47

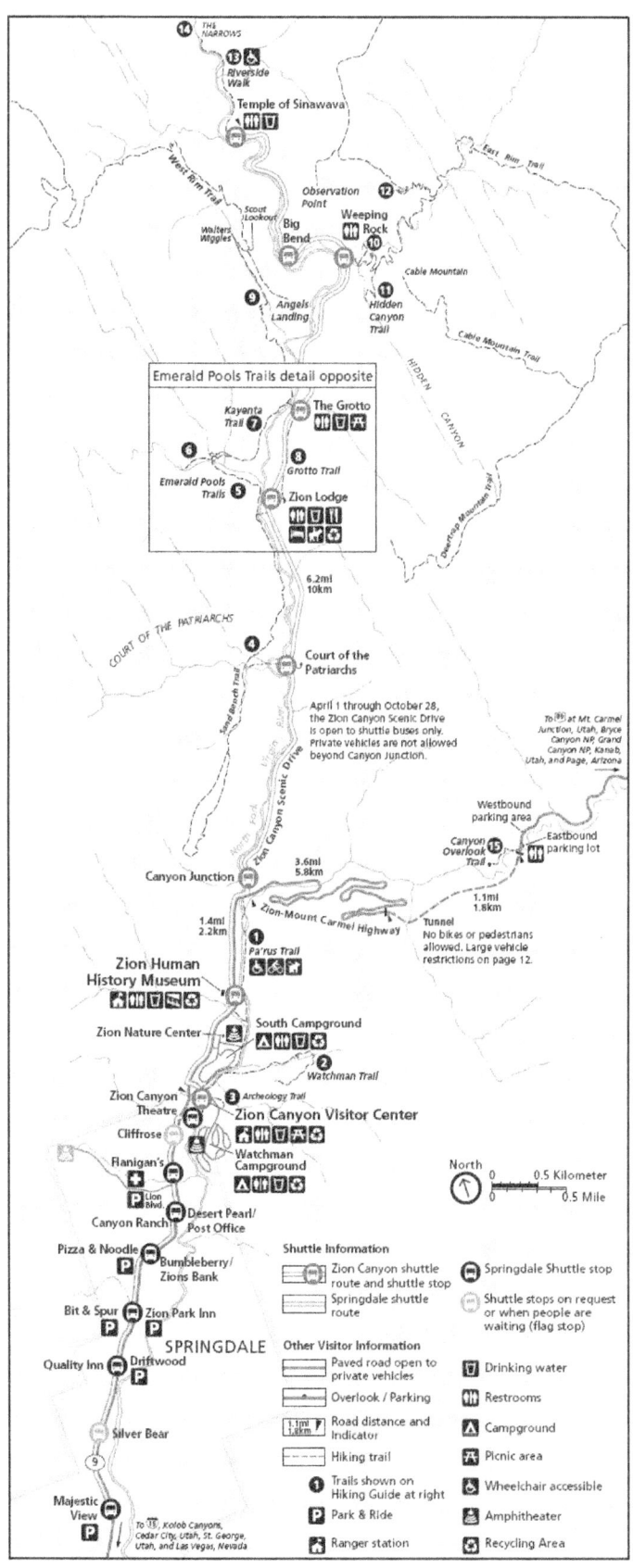

CANYON/RIVER/TRAIL WHERE SITE LOCATED: _____

Please circle the closest body of water:

     Virgin River – East Fork, North Fork   North Creek – Left Fork, Right Fork   La Verkin Creek

     Other: _____

PLEASE GIVE A WRITTEN DESCRIPTION OF WHERE WE SHOULD GO TO FIND THE FOSSIL. THIS IS IMPORTANT INFORMATION WE NEED TO RE-LOCATE THE FOSSIL. PLEASE ANSWER THE FOLLOWING QUESTIONS: Is the site near a road, canyon or visitor use area? Which one? How far is the site from a major landmark? Feel free to draw a map, include UTM Coordinates or a Xerox copy of a topographic map showing the location.

GPS Coordinates: _____   Circle projection (if known): NAD83   NAD27

In what type of terrain was the fossil found?
- a. River bar or dry wash bed
- b. Cliff or slickrock
- c. Valley floor
- d. Talus slope
- e. Other_____

What is the color and texture of the surrounding rock (circle all that apply)?

Color	**Texture**
a. red	a. clayey
b. white/grey	b. popcorn/rough and broken
c. purple/green/yellow	c. sandy
d. other_____	d. banded

Description of the Fossil:

The fossil is (circle all that apply): Bone Tooth Track/Trace Wood Combination   Other: _____

If the fossil is a track, circle the track most similar below.

If the fossil is a bone, what is the general fossil shape?

Contact Information (how can we contact you?):
Name_____
Address_____
Phone or Email: _____
Campground Resident? **Y N** If yes: Site #   (optional) Until when will you be there?

Thank you for your help. If we document the site we will contact you. Please send any photos to fred_armstrong@nps.gov. To report theft or damage call 1-800-227-7286.

STAFF USE ONLY

Notes:

PLEASE RETURN THESE FORMS BY MAIL to Dave Sharrow, Zion National Park, Springdale, UT 84767.

Standard Operating Procedures (SOPs)

Standard Operating Procedure 1
Job Hazard Analysis for Paleontological Fieldwork

This Job Hazard Analysis should be adapted to the conditions of the particular park unit. The park climate will determine whether there are potential hazards from heat exhaustion or hypothermia. The specific dangerous or poisonous animals and plants present at the park should be listed (ie. bears, scorpions, ticks, etc.). Parks may have specific backcountry dangers that need to be added to the Trail Surveys section. Contact your park or regional Safety Officer for assistance.

JOB HAZARD ANALYSIS (JHA)		Date: June 2012	☐ New JHA ☐ Revised JHA	
Park Unit:	Division: Resource Management	Branch:	Location:	
TASK TITLE: Paleontological Fieldwork		JHA Number:	Page _____ of _____	
Job Performed By:	Analysis By: Erica Clites	Supervisor:	Approved By:	
Required Standards and General Notes:	First Aid and CPR			
Required Training:	First Aid and CPR, Defensive Driving			
Required Personal Protective Equipment:	Safety glasses* , hearing protection*, long pants, sun screen, safety vests, respirator* , gloves, hiking boots *Fossil prospecting and Excavation			
Tools and Equipment:	First aid kit, park radio			

Procedures			
Backcountry Trip Plan, Notification of Supervisor or Dispatch, Check in			
Sequence of Job Steps		Potential Hazards	Safe Action or Procedure

54

| Trail and Backcountry Surveys and Monitoring | • Lightning danger, backcountry travel dangers, footing, rockfalls
• Exposure to steep rocky loose terrain with significant hazards for rockfall, rolling rocks, and falls.
• Skin cancer, retinal damage, dehydration/heat exhaustion, hypothermia
• Exposure to poisonous animals and plants | • Prepare Backcountry Trip Plan, notify supervisor of other designate of plans, arrange for check-in with park dispatch, check-in daily and on completion of travel.
• Walk deliberately on trails and beware of tripping hazards
• Use judgment and consider the difficulty of getting assistance to avoid actions that exceed abilities and reason.
• Follow lightning procedures
• Carry radio and extra battery
• Carry map of area
• Bring sufficient clothing, water and food
• Backcountry kits – 10 essentials
• Wear sunglasses and sturdy boots; bring raingear
• Do not climb directly above or below another person. Yell "rock!" if you dislodge anything.
• Take breaks in safe places—check for rockfall and other hazards first.
• Wear a wide-brimmed hat and long pants. Reapply sunscreen (at least SPF 30) multiple times per day. Avoid working at the hottest time of day. On hot days, take frequent breaks.
• Listen for rattlesnakes, flip rocks away from you in case of scorpions. Don't put your hand into crevices.
• Carry epinephrine if predisposed to severe allergic reactions to insect stings. |

Driving / Road Surveys	• Traffic	• Wear orange safety vests • Walk on outside of road shoulder, as far from lane as possible • Make sure traffic sees you
	• Vehicle breakdown	• Proper vehicle maintenance
	• Vehicle accident	• Safe driving practice including following DOI policy for number of hours and what to bring • Wear your seatbelt • Do not use your cell phone for calls or text messages while driving.

Fossil prospecting and Excavation	• Hantavirus or dust inhalation	• Wear respirators when excavating • Identify and avoid packrat middens • Clean respirators after use
	• Leaving tools with the point facing upward or scattered around work site	• Keep tools in a central location and always have the point of tools pointing towards the ground • When handing tools to others, use the handle. Keep any pointed or sharp edges out of the way • Pickup tools before breaks, lunch and at the end of each day • Never place tools in a position where they may cause injury or pose a trip hazard
	• Cuts or punctures with sharp tool edge. Splinters from wood handles.	• Wear eye protection and gloves when using hand tools. Wear safety glasses when using hammer or chisels.
	• Hearing damage	• Wear hearing protection when using power tools.
	• Lifting	• Use power-lift stance, multiple people to lift heavy objects, use proper frame for carrying heavy loads

HAZARD ANALYSIS FORM

Job Hazard Analysis (JHA) is an important accident prevention tool that works by finding hazards and eliminating or minimizing them *before* the job is performed, and *before* they have a chance to become accidents. Use your JSA for job clarification and hazard awareness, as a guide in new employee training, for periodic contacts and for retraining of senior employees, as a refresher on jobs which run infrequently, as an accident investigation tool, and for informing employees of specific job hazards and protective measures. Set priorities for doing JHA's: jobs that have a history of many incidents, jobs that have produced disabling injuries, jobs with high potential for disabling injury or death, and new jobs with no accident history. Here's how to do each of the three main parts of a Job Hazard Analysis:

SEQUENCE OF JOB STEPS

Break the job down into steps. Each of the steps of a job should accomplish some major task. The task will consist of a *set* of movements. Look at the first *set* of movements used to perform a task, and then determine the next logical *set* of movements. For example, the job might be to move a box from a conveyor in the receiving area to a shelf in the storage area. How does that break down into job steps? Picking up the box from the conveyor and putting it on a hand truck is one logical set of movements, so it is one job step. Everything is related to that one logical set of movements is part of that job step.

The next logical *set* of movements might be pushing the loaded hand truck to the storeroom. Removing the boxes from the truck and placing them on the shelf is another logical set of movements. And finally, returning the hand truck to the receiving area might be the final step in this type of job.

POTENTIAL HAZARDS

Identify the hazards associated with each step. Examine each step to find and identify hazards – actions, conditions, and possibilities that could lead to and accident.

It's not enough to look at the obvious hazards. It's also important to look at the entire environment and discover every conceivable hazard that might exist.

Be sure to list health hazards as well, even though the harmful effect may not be immediate. A good example is the harmful effect of inhaling a solvent or chemical dust over a long period of time.

It's important to list *all* hazards. Hazards contribute to accidents, injuries, and occupational illnesses.

In order to do part three of a JHA effectively, you must identify potential and existing *hazards*. That's why it's important to distinguish between a hazard, and accident and an injury. Each of these terms has a specific meaning:

HAZARDS – Potential danger. Oil on the floor is a hazard.

ACCIDENT – An unintended happening that may result in injury, loss or damage. Slipping on the oil is an accident.

INJURY – The result of an accident. A sprained wrist from the fall would be an injury.

SAFE ACTION OR PROCEDURE

Using the first two columns as a guide to decide what actions are necessary to eliminate or minimize the hazards that could lead to an accident, injury, or occupational illness.

Among the actions that can be taken are, 1) engineering the hazard out; 2) providing personal protective equipment; 3) job instruction training; 4) good housekeeping; and 5) good ergonomics (positioning the person in relation to the machine or other elements in the environment in such a way as to eliminate stresses and strains).

List recommended safe operating procedures on the form, and also list required or recommended personal protective equipment for each step of the job.

Be specific. Say *exactly* what needs to be done to correct the hazard, such as, "lift using your leg muscles." Avoid general statements like, "be careful."

Give a recommended action or procedure for *every* hazard.

If the hazard is a serious one, it should be corrected immediately. The JSA should then be changed to reflect the new conditions.

Standard Operating Procedure 2
Documenting a New Paleontological Locality

1) When a new occurrence of fossils in the field is located, first determine whether it should constitute a site. Consider:

   a. Size of the site. Is it large enough to relocate using GPS and photos?

   b. Abundance of fossils. Multiple fossils should generally be present. If only one fossil is present and it is a rare type, it can be established as a site. Also consider the preservation of the fossil (is it exceptionally preserved?) and whether it has a pathology or other interesting component.

   c. Type of fossils. If a common fossil is ubiquitous in the park (ex. permineralized wood, bivalves) this occurrence can be described with special attention given to document unusual occurrences or styles of preservation.

   d. Proximity to established localities. If an established locality of the same fossil type is present within tens of meters of the new occurrence, and is present in the same stratigraphic unit, consider expanding the boundaries of the established site to include the new occurrence.

   e. Guidance from the park's curator or paleontologist. Ideally this subject matter expert will make determinations about the scientific significance of paleontological resources for the park service area and set priorities for site documentation. Notify and consult with the park curator if any specimens are collected. Look at the data in the Integrated Taxonomic Information System (IT IS; http://www.itis.gov/) to confirm all appropriate data is collected with the specimen.

2) If you decide the occurrence does not constitute a site, document it as an isolated find using the form in Appendix D. Complete all fields on the form, take a few photographs and document in your field notebook that you discovered an isolated find.

3) If you have decided to document the occurrence as a new site, first determine the extent of the site. Is it one meter square, ten meters square, or does it constitute a horizon that continues for kilometers? Walk around the site and identify the diversity of fossils present.

4) Complete Paleontological Locality Database Form (Appendix B). Fill out all known fields while present at the site. Assign the site a temporary field number using finders' initials, the year and site number found that year. For example, ECC 2012-01. Later add the park-specific locality number (ex. GLCA 1) or state locality number (ex. 42Ws314t).

5) Take GPS reading at center point of site, or walk perimeter to create a defined area as appropriate (see SOP-7).

6) Take photographs of the site (see SOP-6). Site overviews should be taken in each cardinal direction. Place a backpack or your field assistant at the site center point. Include center point in each photograph. Make sure you can see a landmark on the horizon in at least one of the overviews. Describe on the site forms how to walk to the site, or its location relative to a prominent landmark. Someone should be able to locate the site again using only the photographs.

7) Complete an initial Paleontological Locality Condition Evaluation Form for the site (Appendix C), establishing a baseline for future monitoring. Include in the "Notes" section any specific concerns you identify with natural or human impacts to the site. Make a recommendation for whether the site should be monitored in the future and whether additional documentation of the site is needed (tracksite needs mapping, vertebrate fossils should be cast and collected, latex molds should be made, etc.).

8) In your field notebook, write down the date, time, general location, present weather conditions and name of field assistants (see SOP-5). At a minimum, include that a new site was discovered and documented. Make sure to include the site number. Any observations not included on the site forms should be included in the notebook. If specimens are collected, include what was collected, permit number (if applicable), and field collection or specimen number. If time does not permit complete documentation of the site, recommend a return visit and include directions and photographs.

9) If trackways are present at the site and time permits, consider completing the Trackway Worksheet (Appendix E).

Standard Operating Procedure 3
Monitoring Documented Paleontological Localities

1. Gather the materials needed for field monitoring. Bring the field copy of the site files (see SOP-8) for each site you may visit. Bring extra forms (Appendix B, C, D, E). See list of required and optional gear in Operational Requirements.

2. Relocate the site using the GPS coordinates, photographs, topographic maps, aerial photos and Google Earth or ArcGIS maps provided in site file.

3. Walk around the site, making observations about visitor activity and checking for any damage or changes from previous visits. Compare what you see to previous photos and monitoring forms.

4. Complete the Paleontological Locality Condition Evaluation Form (Appendix D), including the date of the last monitoring visit. Make sure to circle your choice in each category on the form, rather than just recording your total score. Use the photos in the file to note whether fossils are being lost or disturbed. Include in "Comments" any observations from walk-around.

5. A note about completing the monitoring form. For many parks, site monitoring is the main mitigation measure.
   a. The first monitoring form completed for a site provides a baseline before any action is taken. No mitigation measures should be marked.
   b. After the site has been evaluated and included in a cyclic monitoring program, it is appropriate to mark those choices as it applies.
   c. The type of park staff completing the monitoring form also results in different scores. Visitor & Resource Protection staff should determine whether they are actively patrolling an area.

6. Take current photos of the locality photos included in the site file. Make sure you take the photos from the same perspective and at the same scale. If a photo point has been established using a permanent marker or GPS coordinates and an azimuth direction make sure to take the photos from that location. Otherwise, hold the previous photo up and compare it to your view in the camera until they match. These photos will be used to create a long term record of changes at the site in five-, 10-, 25-, 50- and 100 years.
   a. Relocate the *in situ* fossils photographed in the site file. If changes are noticed in fossil condition, note this and take photos.
   b. Describe the photos taken in the log on the back of the monitoring form. Make notes of any changes and describe if new fossils were discovered.
   c. A photograph of the field form for the site as the last photograph from that site can be a useful reference for the later identification and labeling of photographs.

7. Record your visit in your field notebook, including date, others present and what specifically you did while at the site. Also include any recommendation for future work. See SOP-5 for additional information on what should be recorded.

Standard Operating Procedure 4
Prioritizing Paleontological Sites for Monitoring

NOTE: This SOP describes recommendations for how to choose sites for monitoring. All sites should continue to be included in the paleontological site database, even if they are located outside of NPS boundaries or possess little or no locality data.

1. Eliminate sites outside of NPS boundaries. Many databases include sites near parks that may provide useful scientific insights, but are not subject to NPS management. Some sites may require fieldwork to determine whether they are outside of park boundaries. If such sites are on BLM or other governmentally managed property and you note problems with the site, pass on this information to the appropriate person.

2. Eliminate sites with little or no locality data. Often these are historic sites mentioned in literature with only a general description such as "one mile up the Bright Angel Trail" or only a township, range and section. This will not be enough information to relocate the site with any certainty.

3. Eliminate sites with very few or insignificant fossils. Changes at these sites will be difficult to discern over time.

4. Representative monitoring sites can be established for common fossils such as petrified wood. These sites consist of common fossils, but will provide baseline data on natural or human influences on this type of fossil throughout the park. Representative monitoring sites should continue to be monitored.

5. Determine the significance of the site. If prior evaluations of significance have been done, those conclusions may help eliminate Insignificant or Unimportant sites (see Sites to be Monitored in Zion NP section). If the site possesses type specimen quality material, rare material or unusually well-preserved material, it should be considered significant. If a site is determined to be scientifically significant, it should generally be monitored.

6. Susceptibility to erosion. Consider whether the site is susceptible to natural erosion such as catastrophic geohazards or other factors that would cause major degradation or damage of the site. Also consider the site's susceptibility to human disturbance such as development, high potential for vandalism due to easily accessible location and how visitor use in the area may unintentionally affect the site.

7. If the site has been monitored before, and its total score is less than 50, it should continue to be monitored. Management actions may be needed to improve the condition of the site. If the total score is between 50 and 90, it should be considered for monitoring.

8. Logistic considerations. Consider whether the site can be reached in a day's travel and whether it is located close to other sites that will be monitored. Significant sites requiring extended travel can be monitored, but probably only every five years.

9. Determine whether the site in question should be eliminated from consideration or should be incorporated in a monitoring program.

10. Determine the monitoring interval for each site. If sites are subject to theft or vandalism, especially if incidents have already been recorded, sites should be monitored multiple times per year by Visitor & Resource Protection rangers. Sites in poor condition that are susceptible to erosion should be monitored annually. Scientifically significant sites where collections have been made should be monitored annually and any additional fossil material collected. Most sites should be monitored every two to three years, at least initially. After completing three monitoring visits, the monitoring interval should be reevaluated. Sites that are difficult to reach or scientifically significant but with a low risk of erosional impacts should be monitored every five years. Sites that are in excessively unstable locations, where the physical act of accessing the site results in damage to the resource or the creation of a "social trail" that will attract unwanted visitation, should be monitored infrequently.

Standard Operating Procedure 5
Field Notebook Use

These guidelines are provided by John Day Fossil Beds National Monument and are used with permission. You may want to resize some of this information and add it to your field notebook.

Paleontological Field Notes

Field notes should ideally include all of the following information:

- Page Number
- Date
- Where work is being done
- Who is present

> Basic notes for each day's work.

- Field Number
- Taxon
- Element
- In situ / Float
- Locality Description
- Lithology
- Stratigraphic Location
- GPS Coordinates
- Photograph / Orientation
- Airphoto Coordinates
- Notes to preparator / curator

> Specific notes for anything collected or observed and left *in situ*, note the quantity or diversity of *in situ* material.

Basic notes for each day:

Page Number

> All pages in the field notebook must be numbered at the upper outside corner. At JODA we start with the individual's initials, then the last two digits of the year, followed by the page number; these two numbers are separated by a hyphen (example: page 100 in the 2005 notebook of Ted Fremd would be TF05-100). The individual's entire first and last name should be listed as part of each new entry. When a book is completed and a new one begun, the numbering continues. Page numbers only start over every January 1.

Date

> The daily entry should start on a new page and must have the date (placed at the top of the first page).

Where and Who

> The first sentence should contain information regarding *where* work is being done. Include the JDNM locality number and the locality name. This should be followed by *who* else is

present. Especially important is to include the names (or unique initial codes) of the other people who are also keeping notes. Identify non-field crew members by their full name; otherwise archivists in fifty years won't know to which "John" you are referring. It is helpful to include information about where you are working relative to where other people are working. Update this as you move throughout the day.

Why Do Field Notes Matter?

The collection of raw data is the most basic requirement of scientific investigation. Information regarding the cliché who, what, when, where, why, and how is the basis of conclusions in every profession from history to applied science. There are two compelling reasons to take good notes. The first is that good notes will allow a researcher to compile all of the important observations regarding an inquiry into the results and will not miss (or forget) important information when synthesizing conclusions. The second reason, often not fully respected, is that the observations should be reproducible. The scientific method requires that enough information be recorded so that future workers may be able to recreate the same results. This implies an added responsibility to workers in the historical sciences (including paleontology), where specimens are removed from their context. A field collection of fossils is not like an experiment that can be run again. Field notes are not just an aid to synthesizing results; they are themselves a unique record of events and locations that may form the basis of not only the collector's, but also future researchers', conclusions. Therefore, it is imperative that when taking paleontological field notes a worker recognizes that their notes are not just a series of personal scribblings to one's self (to "jog" their own memory later), but that they are a series of instructions and elucidations for *all* potential researchers, including one's self.

Completeness and accuracy

Field notes must be complete and consistent in their format. Any shorthand that is used must be standardized by either the profession as a whole (i.e. UTM coordinate notation) or by the institution doing the collecting (i.e. airphoto coordinate notation). Personal shorthand should be kept to a minimum; what is used should be consistent and explained at the beginning of the notebook. Fieldnotes are documents that will be referenced and utilized by researchers for a long time into the future and we can never fully know with what questions they will assist that researcher. The most important thing to remember is that you will only be one of many people who will be using your field notes.

Additionally, because there is such a great potential that your fieldnotes will be used in support of scientific ideas, it is imperative that all fieldnotes be as accurate as possible. You do not own the fieldnotes,, they are government property and eventually will be included in the park archives. The precision of a measurement should not be more than one significant digit greater than its accuracy. If you are unsure about the geologic unit, say so in your notes. Misidentified specimens can be reidentified if they are properly collected and curated, but an incorrect location may mislead researchers a long time into the future. Entire field expeditions have been devoted to fixing incorrect or incomplete field references. Keep this in mind at all times while in the field.

Finally, falsified locality data is the greatest wrong that may be committed in any field science. Knowingly misrepresenting paleontological field data is never appropriate, even when it is desirable to keep a locality protected from vandalism or theft. It is far better to have incomplete field notes than to have blatantly incorrect notes.

The medium

Notes should be taken at the time an observation is made. Virtually every person who is new to the note-taking process feels compelled to take notes on "scratch" paper and copy the notes into a bound journal at a later time. Copied notes are neater, cleaner, and often times more concise. They are also no longer an accurate record of the events that took place. Scientific note-taking is an event that is recorded by the notes. The notebook then becomes as much an artifact as the specimens that are being discussed. In rare cases where it is appropriate to copy notes into a different notebook, then the original "scratch" paper should be permanently appended to the notebook as well.

Because paleontological notes are usually taken outdoors, all notebooks must have waterproof archival paper. Pens must be waterproof, smudgeproof, fadeproof, and permanent as well. Pencils are appropriate as long as pages are only used on one side so that notes aren't obscured by graphite that may be smudged from one page to its facing page. Additionally, write on only one face of a page if there is a chance that ink may soak through a page (felt-tip marking pens may do this).

Writing notes

Although note-taking protocols may vary from institution to institution and from individual to individual, there are a few pieces of information that ALL field notes should contain:

1. Page numbers: These may be printed in the notebook or may be penned in by hand.
2. Date: The current date should be at the top of any new entry.
3. Location: Where is the work taking place?
4. Workers present: Who is present and who else is taking notes.
5. Type of work: What is being done; prospecting, excavation, section measurement, photography, GPS, etc.

Additionally, information concerning the time of day, weather conditions, and other environmental factors may be recorded.

Correct mistakes by drawing one or two straight horizontal lines through the error ("cross out"), such that the mistake is still legible to the reader. Never scribble or blacken words out. Also never tear pages out of the notebook for other uses. There should not be any question on the part of subsequent readers as to whether information has been removed or censored (a suspicion raised if one sees the nub of a torn page or writing that has been covered up).

Data collection

Appropriate field instrumentation should be used and identified; this includes the type and make of specialized measuring equipment such as GPS units, laser transits, navigation aids, remote sensing devices, etc. Tables, charts, figures, and photographs all may be included. Specific data protocols may vary by situation, institution, and investigation.

Specimen collection

Any object that is collected in the course of scientific investigation must be given a field number that will permanently associate it with the notes that were collected at the same time. There are no exceptions! These may include rocks, bones, fossils, or archaeological relics (**Note**: Collected objects without associated notes are critically limited in their scientific utility.). Even if the importance of an object seems trivial, give it a number. It is easier to discard an object than it is to recreate the conditions under which it was discovered. Field numbers can also be assigned if specimens are not collected; this can be important for understanding the history of investigation at a site. Whenever specimens are collected the park curator should be notified as to the type, number, size and other details of the specimens so they can plan for their inclusion in the park museum collections. If specimens will be sent outside the park for curation, the park curator is responsible for the paper work to track the loan of the specimens.

Field numbers

There are many institutional protocols surrounding the assignment of field numbers. While working at JODA, individuals should follow the protocols outlined here. While working elsewhere, it may be appropriate to follow one of these, or to design your own.

Field numbers usually have identifier initials. These may reflect a person, an institution, or a specific quarry. Generally, an individual who does a lot of collecting and keeps consistent notes will use their own initials. A large group of people representing a single institution for a short period of time (such as a single field expedition or a university class) will use an institutional code. A single quarry that is administered by a single institution may have a unique code associated with all of the specimens from that quarry. In this case there should also be a single notebook associated with the quarry in which all of the specimens are entered. Each entry should be initialed by the person making the notes. If separate notes are also taken, the other notebooks should be referenced in the single "quarry" notebook.

A list of initials is tracked on the "Paleoserver" (P drive) within the "Fieldwork" subfolder of the "SOP" folder in a Microsoft Word file named "FIELD NUMBER INITIALS –" followed by a date corresponding to when it was updated (thus there are a series of these files, so that changes over time can be tracked). New field workers should be assigned a unique set of initials that are recorded in that folder. If your set of initials are taken (both with or without the middle initial), another unique code may be assigned by the supervisor of the field team.

A field number should also have information regarding the year and the chronological order in which the specimens were collected. Additionally helpful is information about the month and locality. A good field number is like an address that allows a curator to figure out when and where a specimen was collected and by whom.

Standard Operating Procedure 6
Photography

Camera Requirements

Digital photographs should be captured at a resolution and quality setting appropriate for the highest detail intended use. Publication quality photos should be taken at a minimum of five megapixels (Baker and Shaw 2012). Because the use of the photo is unknown when it is taken, all photos should be taken with this resolution, or at the highest resolution possible. If the camera will allow, the resolution should be set at 1760 x 1168 or higher. The quality should be set to "super fine" or "high." Uncompressed TIFF or RAW files retain the greatest amount of image information, but are large files which allow fewer images to be saved to any single memory card.

Before leaving for the field, ensure that old photographs are removed from the camera, the camera is functioning properly, the date and time are set correctly, batteries are charged and an extra set is present, the photo resolution is set to maximum, photograph format is set to JPG or TIFF and the camera case is in good shape. Generally it is unnecessary to have the date and time printed on the photo because this data is automatically recorded in the EXIF metadata. Ensure that your camera does record this information before first use. This information can be found in the "properties" of each image.

Site documentation and monitoring can be completed using a range of digital cameras. It is recommended that the camera chosen has a macro setting, which will be the best for photographing individual fossils. A digital SLR with a zoom lens is very helpful for close-up photos when approaching a site directly is not possible (i.e. a dinosaur trackway revealed on the underside of a cliff). A fixed focal-length lens on a digital SLR camera is best for photogrammetry. There are many other considerations when choosing a camera that will not be discussed here.

Scale

Including a scale bar or object of known size in each photograph is very important. The scale you use should be appropriate to the object you are photographing. For example, if you are photographing one brachiopod, you will probably want to use a ten centimeter scale bar. A scale bar with alternating dark and light boxes representing centimeters works well. If you are photographing a dinosaur trackway or outcrop, you should use a meter stick, rock hammer or person for scale.

Lighting

Outdoor photographing is best done mid-morning or just before dusk. The low angle of light tends to bring out details in the body or trace fossils. If you are photographing at mid-day, your photos may be washed out. Photographs with half of the subject in bright light and half in shade are generally not useful, so waiting until lighting conditions change is recommended. Try blocking out some of the light with your body and using a fill-in flash. If you are photographing museum specimens, put them on a flat surface with a black or white background. Use high intensity lights directed from opposite sides to emphasize fossil details.

Photogrammetry

Photogrammetry is where photographs taken with a digital camera are aligned, camera positions are calculated and a three dimensional model is produced (Falkingham 2012). Photogrammetry provides an effective way of documenting fossil sites in great detail. It is rapidly becoming affordable for parks to undertake this work. The three-dimensional models created during this process have many applications for scientific research as well. A recent article describes photogrammetric models created using a standard digital camera and software that is free to download (Falkingham 2012). Even without the required software, parks should consider taking overlapping photographs (at least 50 percent overlapping) for future creation of 3-D models.

Standard Operating Procedure 7
GPS

GPS Requirements

The GPS system currently consists of 25 Department of Defense satellites that orbit the Earth approximately every 12 hours, emitting signals to Earth at precisely the same time (NPS 2011). The position and time information transmitted by these satellites is used by a GPS receiver to trilaterate a location coordinate on the earth using three or more satellites.

All commercially available consumer GPS receivers use the civil-access Standard Position Service (SPS) code. The National Standard for Spatial Data Standard (NSSDA) for 1:24,000 is 13.9 meters at 95% confidence interval. This is also the NPS minimum standard for map data accuracy. Typically even a consumer grade handheld GPS such as Garmin will provide better accuracy than the NSSDA if used carefully. You must monitor the parameter settings described below in order to achieve the appropriate level of accuracy. Points should be recorded in NAD83.

1. Acquire at least four satellites, in order to achieve 3-D position. (In Zion NP some paleontological sites have large portions of the sky obscured by cliffs so obtaining a sufficient number of satellites is often not practical. In these cases: (1) use the trip planning software in the Zion NP GIS office to identify days and times when satellites are most likely to be available, or (2) if GPS is not practical, use visual and topographic features to locate the site manually on GIS layers or topographic maps.)

2. Keep the Positional Dilution of Precision (PDOP) as low as possible, ideally less than four.

3. Most receivers give a field estimate of horizontal error (EHE or EPE), which has shown to be a good indicator of overall positional accuracy.

4. Average only five seconds on points in the open and up to 30-60 seconds under canopy.

5. Ensure 30 seconds of measurement data (file open, GPS receiver on) are collected in the open before and after every point.

6. Set feature settings to 5 – 180 positions, collected at a one second interval and averaged.

7. Use a two-five second interval when walking or driving, recording at least three positions at any change in direction.

See NPS (2011) for specific recommended settings for different types of GPS devices.

Post-processing and Generating ArcGIS Shapefiles

Specific steps for post-processing depend on the GPS unit used. The directions below are generalized and do not include software-specific commands. Differential correction, as described below is recommended, but not required by the NPS Data Standard (NPS 2011). Post-processing improves data accuracy. Real-time differential correction saves both time and money if it is available.

1. Wait at least 24 hours after completion of sampling before differentially correcting a file.

2. Start GPS software and open the GPS job file to be differentially corrected. Select the job file from the appropriate "Corrected" data folder. If you wish, resave the job file as "filename_COR.mmj" in the "Corrected" folder.

3. Download reference station data for the open job file. Differentially correct the data. Ensure that process completes successfully.

4. Export the corrected points to a shapefile for GIS analysis. Save file into the appropriate "Export" folder within your file directory.

5. Rename the exported shapefile to match the job file it originated from. Start ArcCatalog and locate the exported shapefile. Select the file and press F2 to rename it.

Frequently Asked Questions

Q: When should I create a new job file?

> A: It is most efficient to differentially correct one file per day. Remember to note the site or feature name under "Comment." If you record points separated by more than 24 hours it will be more difficult to correct these later. In your program, it may be most appropriate to record a new job file for each locality/site/feature.

Q: How long should I "log" on a point?

> A: If the GPS is in one place, logging on the point longer improves accuracy. If the GPS unit is moving, it is best not to "log" on the point longer than necessary.

Q: Should I have a feature library for my program?

> A: It is useful to set up a feature library for your program if you are recording the same type of data many times. Use the "Feature Library Editor" to make a new feature type. Name your features or design a drop down menu. Create text boxes as needed.

Standard Operating Procedure 8
Data Management

Sensitivity of Data

Specific paleontological locality data is sensitive. Access to this data should be restricted to those who maintain it. If the data is saved on a network drive, it should be restricted to the appropriate staff. All of the types of data discussed below are considered sensitive.

Locality Files and Field Notebook

The data contained in site files needs to be preserved both on paper and electronically. Paper site files should be filed in separate folders and kept in a secure (locked) location. Original forms should never be taken in the field. Make copies of site forms for field use. Field use forms are best kept in clear page protectors (one page protector per site). Field use files will need to be kept up-to-date, and the most recent monitoring forms replaced. This will help keep papers together in the field and prevent some weather damage. Parks should consider archiving paper site files at some point.

All original site forms should also be scanned to PDF or saved as modified Microsoft Word files on the appropriate network drive. Locality data can either be separated by data type (i.e. site form, photographs, GPS) or kept together with one folder for each locality. It is possible to include links to scanned forms in a Microsoft Access site database.

The field notebook should be periodically scanned to PDF or copied to ensure that no data is lost in the field. At the completion of each field notebook, the entire notebook should be scanned to PDF format. See more guidelines about field notebook use in SOP-5.

Original field notebooks, and all related data will eventually become part of the park's archives managed by the park curator, discuss with them protocols for transferring these materials to the park archives.

Site Database

In addition to site files, it is helpful to have a Microsoft Excel or Access database to store and display all site data for the park in one location. Zion NP currently uses an Excel database. The Utah Geological Survey (UGS) designed an Access database that has been adapted for use by some parks. Database fields should match site forms to ensure consistent entries. Microsoft Access has enhanced sorting capabilities from Excel, as well as forms that can be created to facilitate data entry and output. Microsoft Access is the National Park Service standard database software.

UGS is presently working on an internet-based MySQL system for the Bureau of Land Management that links to ArcGIS. Database templates can be provided upon request. Please contact Vincent Santucci for more information (Phone: 202-513-7186; Email: Vincent_Santucci@nps.gov).

GPS and GIS Data

Each park should have standards for storing and organizing GPS and GIS data. If official standards have not been established, communicate with other Resource Management staff and try to follow their established methods.

One suggested file structure for storing GPS data is as follows:
  Base: Files downloaded from Reference Station
  Corrected: Job files that have been differentially corrected
  Export: Shape files to load into ArcGIS
  Raw: Job files recorded in field

GIS data is best organized in geodatabases. A separate geodatabase should be created for paleontology, given the sensitive nature of the data. The location of paleontological resources on NPS property cannot be released to the general public. Within the park, site data should be available only to park staff maintaining it.

Your park may choose to input locality data directly in the field using data dictionaries. This requires a more advanced GPS device, but eliminates errors that may be introduced during data entry by using drop down menus. It is important to establish quality control methods to ensure the accuracy of entries before adding them to the locality database/geodatabase. If data dictionaries are used, paper forms should still be brought into the field in case of equipment failure.

Photographs and Metadata

Photos taken during site documentation and monitoring are project data that need to be organized, documented and preserved in conjunction with all other project data (Baker and Shaw 2012). The generation of hundreds of digital photos requires consistency in downloading, naming, editing and creating metadata. After images have been acquired, a digital photograph workflow should follow these general steps:

1. Establish directory structure and destination
  These guidelines use folders titled: Original, Edited, PDF and Misc.

2. Download original photos from camera
  Downloaded photos need to be preserved in their original form because many photo editing programs will automatically destroy the photographic metadata imprinted to the picture file by the camera. After saving original photos to the /Original folder, the directory should be set to "read-only" permission to prevent accidental edits.

3. Copy original photos for editing
  Save the copies to the /Edited folder.

4. Review photos
  Identify data vs. non-data photos. Non-data photos are incidental or opportunistic photos and not part of a well-defined data collection protocol. Non-data photos should be moved to the /Misc directory. Delete lower quality duplicate photos at this point.

5. Rename photos

Image file names should not use spaces or special characters and should be less than 20 characters in length. Separate the components of a file name with underscores. Use software to batch rename photos to conform to your chosen format. For example, YYYY.ProjectNumber.FrameNumber_ImageDescription or PhotographerName_SiteNumber_YYYYMMDD_PhotoID. Naming conventions should conform to existing park-level guidance.

6. Attach metadata

The National Park Service has a Digital Photo Metadata Standard (DPMS) that includes seven mandatory metadata elements that are required to discover, interpret and manage an image. These are: Title; Image_Content_Place; Image_or_Set_Create_Data; NPS_Unit_Alpha_Code; Metadata_Access_Constraints; Constraints_Information; and Contact_Organization. For more information and a detailed description of mandatory and optional fields see: http://npsfocus.nps.gov/docs/guide/metadata/MetadataStandards.html Metadata can be attached using software such as GPS Photo Link.

7. Edit and proof if necessary

Rotate photos to their appropriate orientation.

8. Convert format

Some photos should be collected for inclusion in digital site file records. This decision should be made by personnel familiar with paleontological field methods, sites at the particular park and ideally someone who has completed multiple monitoring cycles at those sites. Selected images can be added to a site specific photo record form and converted to PDF format. The PDF file will be saved with other site data on the network drive. The site specific photo record form should be printed on archival photo paper and filed with the paper site files.

Photographs, and all related data will eventually become part of the park's archives managed by the park curator. Discuss with the curator protocols for transferring these materials to the park archives.

NPS 116/117670, November 2012